G *m*

Dr. Fuchsia T. Pickett

Destiny Image Publishers
P.O. Box 351
Shippensburg, PA 17257-0351

"We Publish the Prophets"

ISBN 1-56043-028-1

For Worldwide Distribution
Printed in the U.S.A.

First Printing: 1991
Second Printing: 1991
Third Printing: 1993

Acknowledgments

I am deeply grateful . . .

To **Pastors Samuel and Paulette Farina** of Christian Assembly, Columbus, Ohio and their gracious parishioners, for being the first to invest monetarily in the project of publishing *God's Dream.*

To my pastor, **Sue Curran** of Blountville, TN; **Rev. Mark Chironna** of Raleigh, NC; **Dr. Myles Monroe** of the Bahamas, and **Dr. Judson Cornwall**, for insisting that I write what God has deposited in my heart and life during the past several years.

To **Dr. Judson Cornwall**, my spiritual brother, colaborer, and friend for editing the manuscript and offering counsel. To **Carol Noe** for her untiring labor in preparing, processing and typing the original manuscript.

Dedicated to my husband, Leroy.

It takes a "special man" of strength, security and stamina to be the husband of a woman minister, teacher and writer. Leroy is that man. Though he does not speak publicly, he functions invaluably in our ministry, especially in the production of manuals, tapes and books. The message he preaches in the living of his life is one of total commitment to the mandate God has laid upon our lives. I am grateful to God for his love, encouragement and total support.

Contents

Foreword

In the mid-seventies, I invited a woman evangelist to my church for a weekend. Fuchsia Pickett's ministry was so electrifying that we extended her stay for three weeks. She used our church for many months as her headquarters while God directed her ministry through various churches on the West Coast. It was the beginning of a friendship that has become a brother/sister relationship in the Lord.

Our roles were reversed many years later when I made my headquarters in her church in Plano, Texas. For several of those years, I served as an assistant pastor to the congregation. Now God has again released Fuchsia Pickett to the larger body of Christ as a mother in Israel. Her academic background and years of experience as a teacher, evangelist and pastor have given her insights desperately needed in the Church today.

This book is the heart of the message that God has burned into the soul of this precious woman. She has envisioned the reality of God's eternal plan. When people embrace this truth, it becomes life-changing. I have heard her share these principles in many different situations, and it has always produced life and inspired action.

If this book can accomplish the same results that miraculously occur when she presents these truths in person, it will become a channel for revitalizing pastors, elders, deacons and lay workers. In turn, the entire Church will be revived. Read this book with a prayerful attitude and allow God to effect changes in you. Study the principles shared and search them out in your Bible.

I highly commend the author to you as a woman of the Word, a person of integrity and one who lives what she preaches.

Judson Cornwall, Th.D.
Phoenix, Arizona

Introduction

Peter declared on the day of Pentecost what had been prophesied by Joel: "... in the last days, saith God, I will pour out of my Spirit upon all flesh: and your sons and daughters shall prophesy, and your young men shall see visions, and your old men shall *dream dreams* ..." (Acts 2:17) In the original language the phrase "old men" does not refer to age or gender, but rather to *mature saints*. The understanding is that when God begins to pour out of His Spirit, mature saints will know the dream of God's heart and the young men and women will grasp portions of the vision and run to fulfill it as they see the eternal plan that was predestined by the Council of God before the foundation of the world.

The connotation of the word "dream" as used in *God's Dream* is to have aspirations, hopes, ideals and longings for the future. A dream is thus a visionary hope that creates deep longing for its fulfillment. That intense desire becomes a motivating force for action. God's dream filled His heart with longing and motivated Him to realize its fulfillment.

What was God's dream? The great heart of God had a dream that was born out of His need. Although some theology teaches that God has no need because of the fact of His self-existence, I believe, by definition, we can establish that God had a need. God is love. Love needs someone who can become a recipient, one who can respond to that love. In order to meet that need, God had a *dream* for a family that would be made in His Image, and into whom He could pour Himself.

Having determined to have a family, the Triune Godhead took a sworn covenant among Themselves that that dream would be fulfilled, judicially setting full redemption to our account before mankind was ever created or time established. How incalculable must have been the suffering endured when Jesus became the Lamb, slain in the heart of God from the foundation of the world (Rev. 13:8)! The Godhead had to suffer that *hurt-love* in order for His dream to become a reality. That sacrificial love initiated the fulfillment of God's eternal plan to bring many sons into glory.

The Scriptures give glimpses of this wonderful plan from earliest history. However, that covenant dream was not completely unveiled until God revealed the mystery of the Church to the apostle Paul who declared ". . . the mystery, which from the beginning of the world hath been hid in God . . ." (Eph. 3:9) God's dream unveils His eternal plan, revealing what He has done, is now doing and will do. His desire for a family is destined to be fulfilled. God will have a family in His own Image, revealed through Jesus, the express Image of His Person. It is the author's prayer that every reader will determine to become a part of fulfilling God's dream for mankind.

1

The Cost of God's Dream

The Hurt-love of God

Truth has the incredible power to free man of despair, hopelessness and a meaningless existence, and to create in him a sense of destiny and purpose that can motivate him to greatness. Jesus said of Himself, "I am the truth" (John 14:6). To believe in Jesus involves receiving the truth of His teachings and allowing them to change our thinking, our values and our behavior. Lies that are working in our lives to destroy us are only exposed as they are contrasted with truth. In the light of truth, those lies lose their seductive power and we are set free from their destruction. Freedom is the scriptural promise to all

1

who walk in truth. "You shall know the truth, and the truth shall make you free" (John 8:32). That promise gives each of us hope to become the person God intended us to become as we walk in His truth. Only as we pursue truth can we expect to know real meaning and purpose for our individual lives, our homes and our churches.

There is a dynamic truth in the Bible that has been pivotal to my life. I was not aware of this powerful truth, despite the fact that I had finished my graduate studies in theology and for my thesis had rewritten the 500 cardinal doctrines. Through my studies, I had learned how to investigate the great truths of the Bible and thought I knew something about almost every doctrine. I prided myself on my attempts to be an exegetical theologian, pastoring and carefully teaching the Word in Bible colleges for seventeen years. However, after receiving the baptism of the Holy Spirit, which brought me into a greater relationship with the divine Teacher, I discovered one of the great truths of the Bible that I had never seen before. I didn't know that the destiny of my life hinged on understanding God's eternal plan, which He unveiled to man through His hurt-love.

An understanding of God's eternal plan for mankind provides the answers to the five innate questions found in the heart of every person ever born. The lonely existence of all humanity evokes the five-fold cry:

"Who made me? Who is God? What is the purpose of my life? How can I fulfill my destiny? After this life, what?" These questions are so simple that we stumble over them, yet so profound that if we cannot answer them we simply exist, without any true sense of direction or meaning for our lives. Until we properly answer these questions we do not know we are people of destiny, born at the exact time God intended that we be born. When we discover answers to these questions, our search for identity is over. We know who God is and who He meant us to be.

As soon as children are old enough to ask questions, they begin to wonder where they came from and Who made them. Many do not receive satisfactory answers to these questions in the schools or churches they attend. As teenagers they may turn to drugs, promiscuous sex, even suicide, searching desperately for their identity. (I do not believe anyone would ever commit suicide who understood the truth of God's eternal plan.) Later, as college students, their professors offer them various philosophies in an attempt to answer these basic questions, without success. Still searching for truth, many turn to Eastern religions, hoping to find answers that will satisfy their hearts' cry. Failing to find the answers they seek, which cannot be found apart from knowing God, many people live in a frustration that ends in hopelessness and despair.

A man in my congregation in Texas acknowledged that the extraordinary success he was enjoying in his life and career was because of his understanding of God's eternal plan. He had attained to everything a man could want before he reached the age of forty. In his address to a distinguished audience on the occasion of accepting the presidency of a large corporation, he declared, "I received my training and degrees from a university, but I did not prepare for this position through my university training. The teaching of my pastor, who showed me God's eternal plan, put my life on pivot. I am prepared to take this position because I know Who made me, who I am, why I am here, and how this position relates to those issues." His life was given purpose by his understanding of God's eternal plan for him.

What does that plan involve, and how does the understanding of it influence the destiny of a life? To answer that question, let's allow our imaginations to take us back into the eons of eternity, to the "beginning," to listen to the triune Godhead as They expressed a deep desire among Themselves. Because of Who God is, He had a need. Though our theological understanding of God's self-existence, which pictures God as having need of nothing, often prevails in our thinking, all Scripture testifies to the contrary, showing us that God had a need. God is love (I John 4:8). Love is not merely an attribute of God's character, but the essence of His Being. The nature of love requires a recipient, one who will respond by choice to the love given. Because God is love, He needed someone to respond to His love. Because of that longing, They said among Themselves, "Let us make man in our image" (Gen. 1:26). God expressed His need in His desire for a family, one into whom He could pour His very nature. His purpose in creating mankind was to have someone with whom to fellowship and share His love. He desired a family who would have His "family spirit" and would choose to respond to His love. He did not create a robot to love Him automatically, for, by definition, love does not force someone to respond with love. God wanted a family who would choose to love Him.

In eternity, the three members of the Godhead took an inter-theistic covenant and swore among Themselves that God's dream would be fulfilled. They became totally involved in bringing that covenant to pass, to fulfill God's dream for a family. God later revealed this covenant to Abraham, as the Book of Hebrews tells us: "When God made promise to Abraham, because he could swear by no greater, he sware by himself..." (Heb. 6:13) God needed no man to swear by; They swore by each other. Having confirmed the covenant with an oath in eternity, the triune Godhead had initiated among Themselves Their dream for a family.

There was equality among the three members of the Godhead in eternity, as we understand when we read of Christ Jesus "who . . . thought it not robbery to be equal with God" (Phil. 2:6). Again we read, "In the beginning was the Word, and the Word was with God, and the Word was God" (John 1:1). However, God's plan for a family would affect that equality as the Father looked beyond Adam's disobedience to make provision for the redemption of mankind, whom They were going to create in Their image. God's eternal plan was decreed, willed, purposed and predestined before man was created. In the corridors of eternity, Jesus came out of the Godhead as the Son of God, suffering His *kenosis* to become the "Lamb slain from the foundation of the world" (Rev. 13:8). That emptying of Himself of which we read in the second chapter of the Book of Philippians happened first in eternity.

It cost the Godhead inestimable suffering to bring Their love to us. One of our favorite Bible verses reveals the pain involved in bringing God's love to man. As children we learn to quote, "For God *so loved* the world, that he gave his only begotten Son, that whosoever believeth in him should not perish, but have everlasting life" (John 3:16). This is a statement of hurt-love. We cannot comprehend the suffering of God in eternity. Knowing that, because man would fail the love test, Jesus would have to become the sacrificial Lamb to redeem us unto Himself, God suffered that incalculable loss. Yet so great was God's need for someone into whom He could pour His love that He proceeded to fulfill His dream to have a family.

God's hurt-love produced the nature of the Lamb. His family would share His nature, the Lamb Spirit of hurt-love. Jesus came, not to save us from hell, but to give the Father a family that would reflect the nature of the Father's love. To accomplish that purpose, Jesus became the Lamb of God, slain in the heart of God. In the types of the Old Testament, we see the suffering heavenly Father each time a man had to choose his own spotless lamb, tie it with a cord and take it to the Temple to offer it as a sacrifice. He is walking with that prepared pascal lamb, tied with a cord; He comes with a hurt-love, bringing His Lamb to slaughter in order to redeem us. God's heart is beating with a longing to impart to us the same quality of love the Godhead enjoyed in eternity. Is it any wonder the highest order of worship found in the Book of the Revelation is expressed in the cry, "Worthy is the Lamb that was slain to receive power, and riches, and wisdom, and strength, and honour, and glory, and blessing" (Rev. 5:12)?

God gave us a beautiful eight-fold picture of His Lamb in the Scriptures to portray vividly His plan of redemption of mankind. The apostle Peter wrote: "Redeemed . . . with the precious blood of Christ, as of a lamb without blemish and without spot: who verily was foreordained before the foundation of the world" (I Pet. 1:18-20). Peter showed us the lamb of *predestination*. We see the lamb of *paradise* in the Garden of Eden, where blood was shed to clothe Adam and Eve with animal skins. From then on, all sacrificial offerings looked back to the one made by Jehovah-Jesus in the Garden of Eden, and forward to the sacrifice Christ was to make on Calvary. Abraham and his son, Isaac, discovered the *lamb of promise* after they ascended the slopes of Mount Moriah to worship. Isaac asked his father, "Where is the lamb for a burnt offering?" Abraham answered, "God will provide himself a lamb for a burnt offering" (Gen. 22:8). The *passover lamb* was revealed to the children of Israel on the night when the death angel visited the first-born of Egypt (Exodus 12). When John the Baptist saw Jesus coming to the Jordan and declared, "Behold the Lamb of God, which taketh away the sin of the world" (John 1:29), he alluded to the lamb the Hebrews offered as a sacrifice every morning and evening in their ritual of worship—the *lamb of pardon*. The *lamb of propitiation* was revealed in the Hebrews' celebration of the Day of Atonement. The *lamb of prophecy* was seen by Isaiah when, under the prophetic inspiration of the Holy Spirit, he declared, "he is brought as a lamb to the slaughter" (Isa. 53:7). Finally, on the historical cross of Calvary, we saw the *lamb provided*. In the Lord Jesus, God fulfilled every promise, every prophecy, every sacrificial type found in the Bible. That day at Calvary, the Father was still leading His Lamb, all the way to the cross, to bring His dream to pass.

The most wonderful love story ever told is the story of God's love. All mankind is part of God's dream for a family, "according as he hath chosen us in him before the foundation of the world . . . having predestinated us unto the adoption of children by Jesus Christ to himself, according to the good pleasure of his will" (Eph. 1:4-5). Every person who would ever be born was in God's mind in eternity when He initiated that dream. Our names were not written in the Lamb's Book of Life when we received Jesus as our Savior. They were written there before the foundation of the world. From eternity God willed that no person on earth should perish. He recorded every name. God said to Jeremiah the prophet, "Before I formed you in the womb I knew you" (Jer. 1:5). The psalmist David declared, "My frame was not hidden from you when I was made in the secret place. When I was woven together in the depths of the earth, your eyes saw my unformed body. All the days ordained for me were written in your book before one of them came to be" (Ps. 139:15-16, NIV). God knew us before we were born, and ordained that we would have life. Our names will only be blotted out of the Lamb's Book of Life if we do not choose to have the life of God. In the Book of the Revelation we read, "He that overcometh, the same shall be clothed in white raiment; and I will not blot out his name out of the book of life . . ." (Rev. 3:5) If we choose to be part of God's family, our names will remain in the Book of Life. If we do not, they will be blotted out. He chose us in Him before the foundation of the world. It is up to us to choose Him now in order to enjoy the eternal life He has provided.

Having purposed to fulfill His dream for a family in spite of the cost, God began to unfold His eternal plan by cutting an eon in half and calling it time. He began His work of creation and set mankind in the Garden of Eden. There He fellowshipped with the first ones He created to become the family that would satisfy His heart of love and fulfill His dream. But Adam and his wife failed the love test through their disobedience. The Voice came walking, seeking him. "Adam, where are you?" Still the Father's dream, known only to the Godhead, was not revealed to man. God couldn't tell Adam of the covenant of the Godhead because of his disobedience.

Centuries later, Moses received the law of God, but that law could not tell us what God's dream was. That which was in God's heart—His dream—was not revealed. The historians, psalmists and poets of the Bible did not perceive it. Even the prophets were not aware of God's dream. Four hundred dark years after the prophets were silent, what God had planned was not yet revealed.

So God cut out His love in the form of a Person and sent Him to earth as the express image of God. Everything Jesus did, each word He spoke, was to show us the Father's heart. Jesus healed the sick and set the captives free to reveal to us the Father's love. However, just before Jesus left this earth, one of His disciples asked Him to show them the Father; then they would be satisfied. We can almost hear the disappointment in Jesus' answer to His disciples. "Have I been so long time with you, and yet hast thou not known me? He that hath seen me hath seen the Father" (John 14:9).

Even Jesus could not tell His disciples what was in the Father's heart. They had centered their thoughts on a present earthly kingdom. Jesus said to them, "I have yet many things to say unto you, but ye cannot bear them now" (John 16:12). He told them He was returning to the Father so that the Counselor could come. The Holy Spirit was part of the plan; He was not an afterthought. He would move inside them and enlighten their minds. "When he, the Spirit of truth, is come, he will guide you into all truth . . . he shall receive of mine, and shall shew it unto you" (John 16:13-14).

Jesus completed the plan for the redemption of mankind through His sacrifice on Calvary. The Holy Spirit was then entrusted to do His precious work in the earth to draw men to God. His task was to put into us what Jesus brought—that heartbeat. The throb of God's heart was still to have a family in His image, with His family spirit—the Spirit of the Lamb—to live and rule with Him. However, no one had yet been able to declare that dream fully to us. On the day of Pentecost, when the Holy Spirit came, Peter put his telescope to the entire Church Age, but he didn't see the whole dream of God. He saw bits of its beginning and ending as he prophesied (Acts chapter two), but he didn't say a word about what was in the Father's heart.

Then one day, a man with a slaughtering spirit, seemingly farther from the heart of God than anyone could be, had a supernatural encounter with the living God, and was apprehended for a special purpose. Saul of Tarsus was converted and became Paul, the apostle. He was a "full gospel preacher" for a while, until God told him to go to the desert of Arabia. Without conferring with flesh and blood, he obeyed the Spirit's command. During the three years Paul spent in that desert, the Father unfolded to him the mystery that had been hidden since before the foundation of the world.

Paul explained to the church at Ephesus that God's eternal plan was ". . . to make plain to everyone the administration of this mystery, which for ages past was kept hidden in God . . . His intent was that now, through the church, the manifold wisdom of God should be made known to the rulers and authorities in the heavenly realms, according to his eternal purpose which he accomplished in Christ Jesus our Lord" (Eph. 3:9-11, NIV). God was going to realize His dream for a family through the Church, the body of Christ on the earth.

Throughout Paul's christological epistles, he reveals the purpose of God for the Church. God will have a glorious Church that will bear His image, with each Christian fulfilling his part of forming the family that God desires. Paul declared:

> *. . . speaking the truth in love, we will in all things grow up into him who is the Head, that is, Christ. From him the whole body, joined and held together by every supporting ligament, grows and builds itself up in love, as each part does its work* (Eph. 4:15-16).

It seems almost too good to be true that God will have a family as described by Paul, especially when we are living in homes and churches that seem to be full of "spots and wrinkles." Why is there such a disparity between what God intends for His family and who we are now? Where is the unity, the love, the Christ-like humility that is to characterize the Church? The answers to these questions will help us to close the gap between God's dream for a family that will reflect His nature and the people we are today. We must believe that God's dream will be fulfilled as He purposed it from eternity. He has promised, "I will put my laws in their minds and write them on their hearts. I will be their God, and they will be my people. No longer will a man teach his neighbor, or a man his brother, saying, 'Know the Lord,' because they will all know me, from the least of them to the greatest" (Heb. 8:10b-11, NIV). If we pursue the truth about ourselves and allow the Holy Spirit to set us free from those characteristics and flaws of our sinful natures that keep us from reflecting the nature of Christ in our lives, we will become part of fulfilling God's dream in the earth.

When we were made, we were neither moral nor immoral, but were created amoral. We had to make a choice. God knew before He made us that man would fail the test of love and make the wrong choice. He also knew that if He sent His love and placed it within us, He could give us the family spirit of God. We cannot get that *family* spirit from anyone else.

Reality tells us that we are not born in the image of God as in the original creation. We still have the potential for that image—we still have a spirit. However, our human spirit is dead because of Adam's sin. We have a soul made up of a mind, a will and emotions. The Bible says our minds are carnal (Rom. 8:7) and our wills are rebellious (Isa. 53:6). Did you ever see a baby say "yes" before he said "no"? Experience tells us that our emotions are self-centered and warped. We concern ourselves more with how we are offended than we do with how we offend. All these human traits are contrary to the family spirit of God. So our spirits need to be made alive to God and our souls need to be redeemed. We were created in the image of God, but we lost that image through Adam's disobedience.

Through disobedience God's dream was silenced. We cannot be in love with God without walking in obedience to Him. Jesus said, "If ye love me, keep my commandments" (John 14:15). What helped me learn to obey God was that I learned to love and to obey my daddy. His love for me motivated me. For example, he instilled in me the beauty of being virtuous, to the extent that if a boy had insulted me, I would have slapped him. My daddy inspired me by telling me how proud he was going to be to see me walk down the aisle as a virtuous young bride. I never went on a date without thinking about my daddy's advice. I had a little taste of what motivating love is—to do my daddy's will. Babies don't know who their daddies are. All they know is their daddies' provision. As children grow up, there comes a time when they love to obey their daddies. They begin to know him and to ask how they can help him, becoming more involved in his interests. The heavenly Father wants us know Him as our Father. His whole purpose is that we might love Him, and prove that love through our obedience to Him.

If we are to come into obedience to the commands of God, we have to be willing to suffer. Because our natures are contrary to the nature of God, the process of becoming like Him will cause suffering to our souls. When His will crosses ours, we begin to understand what it means to deny ourselves, take up the cross and follow Him. We must choose to give up our *ways*, our *will*, our *work*, our *walk*, our *words*, our *worship* and our *warfare*. We must be willing to exchange our sinful natures for the nature of God. This process of being changed into His image requires the work of the cross in each of our lives, daily allowing the Holy Spirit to change us.

In Moses' Tabernacle, which is a type of our "temple," the furniture was laid out in the shape of a cross. It speaks of the price redemption cost and of what the Father suffered to change us into His image. Everything God made that has breath has a cross displayed in it. My face has a cross in it; my body forms a cross. Love came by way of the cross. We will experience the work of the cross in our lives if we respond in obedience to His love.

Many Charismatic teachers deny the need for suffering. They have taught us to rebuke everything the cross brought, to confess that we don't have to have anything that hurts or cuts away our self-lives. They don't want to talk about the fourth baptism. We speak eagerly of the baptism into the body of Christ, water baptism, and the baptism in the Holy Spirit. The baptism of suffering, however, is not as readily taught. We don't want to suffer. We love to sing the words of the hymn ". . .at the cross where I first saw the light." However, our position now is not "at" the cross. After we have seen the light, we change positions. Home is "in" the cross. Paul said, "God forbid that I should glory, save *in* the cross of our Lord Jesus Christ" (Gal. 6:14). There is no way home without allowing the cross to destroy the self-life so that we can receive the family spirit of God.

Too often we find ourselves exalting the self-life. When man is lacking the principles of true revelation, he will seek only that love which benefits him. Much of our preaching has emphasized what God can *give* us. Even in receiving salvation, we understand that Jesus saves us from sin and from hell, but we need to know more about God than just receiving His benefits. The Spirit reveals to the creature in Christ that God's *Being* is pre-eminent over His *doing*. Who He is is more significant than what He does. What He does is for the purpose of our seeing Who He is. Do we measure our love for Him by what He does for us? If we do, then we are not involved in Who He is. God is love, and as we have seen, that love involves suffering. Jesus said ". . . anyone who does not take his cross and follow me is not worthy of me. Whoever finds his life will lose it, and whoever loses his life for my sake will find it" (Matt. 10:38-39, NIV). He promised us that a cross was involved in our knowing His love, but said that was the way to find life.

Jesus' love for us eventually led Him to Calvary. Where do we think our love for Him will lead us? As we lay down our selfish desires and allow God's love to be reflected in our natures, the world will see our love for God and for one another. Then they will believe in Jesus (John 17:21). This is my opinion, but I don't think we are going to demonstrate much of God's love until we experience some hurt-love. We are not God, but He is our Father; if we are to reflect His nature, then we must know the love that came out of pain—a love that suffered supreme cost. It is an unselfish love that loves at any price. Paul cried, "that I may know him, and the power of his resurrection, and the fellowship of his sufferings . . ." (Phil. 3:10) He understood that suffering was an integral part of knowing God's love.

How can we experience that love if we are not willing to take up our own cross? How will we go home with His kind of hurt-love without experiencing death to the self-life? Jesus suffered the loss of everything He had in the Godhead to bring His love to us. Yet we aren't willing to suffer a little crucifixion of our selfish desires, but would rather preach "self-esteem" and "my rights." That is not the heartbeat of God or His nature.

One of the six requirements Jesus laid down for discipleship is that we love Him above everything else. That requires our allowing the cross to destroy our love of self. Walking in obedience to the commands of God, we must deny the sinful propensities in our wills, minds and emotions. That is bearing the cross daily as Jesus instructed us to do. The Holy Spirit changes my decisions, thoughts and desires, causing me to fulfill God's pleasure in my life. What I take to the cross in death will come forth in life on the other side of the cross. I demonstrate that life in my love for God reflected in my obedience to Him.

There is an earnest cry being born in many hearts to know who God is. I believe the next move of God is going to unveil the heavenly Father as we have never known Him. Who is my Father? He is love. We must respond to His hurt-love by being willing to carry our cross and lose our self-life, to become conformed to His image. Can you imagine the joy of the Father when He sees the family come home as He dreamed? His very heartbeat expressed the desire to have a family in His Image, with His Spirit and His Nature, one who loves Him with His kind of love: *hurt-love*.

God's eternal plan will be realized in our individual lives, in our homes, and ultimately in the Church as we are conformed to the image of Christ through the working of the Holy Spirit in us. If we are to be part of God's dream, we will need to cultivate a relationship with the Holy Spirit, understanding Who He is and cooperating with Him as He works to fulfill God's dream for mankind.

2

The Confirmation of God's Dream

Knowing the Holy Spirit

When Jesus told His disciples that He would return to the Father and send the Holy Spirit to teach them all things (John 14:26), He was actually revealing the next phase of God's dream. The Holy Spirit had been entrusted with the task of ultimately bringing the family of God home, changed into the Image of God. In eternity, this third Person of God had suffered his *kenosis* and chosen to become a Servant to do His part to bring a family back to the Father.

There have been many outpourings of the Holy Spirit since the day of Pentecost, as the Servant has been faithful in His part of fulfilling God's eternal plan. In every move of God, the Holy Spirit has restored truths to the Church and empowered men and women to declare the gospel in a way that has resulted in great ingatherings of souls. However, I believe there is coming an outpouring of the Holy Spirit such as we have never seen before. If we meet the conditions, we are going to be part of the fulfillment of God's Word, which promises that the earth will be filled with the knowledge of the glory of the Lord as the waters cover the sea (Hab. 2:14).

In 1963, while I was ministering in a church in Klamath Falls, Oregon, the Lord spoke to me, saying that if I would stay in His Presence, He would show me what was going to happen in the Church and what He was going to do in the world when He poured out His revival. So I waited there in prayer, and He took me into the heavenlies and let me see the revival that is coming. I saw it more clearly than I see the faces of men.

The Holy Spirit used the analogy of a hydroelectric power plant to explain to me what He was doing. (I knew nothing about electricity—I couldn't have fixed a light switch if my life depended upon it.) Hour after hour He carried me in the heavenlies, showing me heaven's *dunamis*. In the heavens above the Church, God was doing the excavation for the building of a huge power plant. I saw how carefully He laid the foundation, and how exactly He measured the sand that went into it. He cleansed everything and placed every screen and tube in order precisely as they should be. Then He ran the prime lines, the primary lines, and the secondary lines out through transformers.

As I watched, I saw that the power came down through the Church. Jesus is the Head of the Church, and He was holding this gigantic power plant in His hands. From the Church His power flowed throughout all the world. I saw five geographical locations in the United States where there would be vital hubs, and God would dig many deep reservoirs, connecting pipes together, as "deep was calling unto deep" (Ps. 42:7). The Holy Spirit was creating a network of churches into which He would pour His Spirit after digging them out, creating fountains out of which would flow living water. "Deep" would call to another "deep," until there was a great network of churches filled with living water. When everything was in order, I saw that He was going to pull a great switch and send an "old-fashioned, heaven-sent, sky-blue, sin-killing, gully-washing" revival. Then I heard the water begin to run. I knew the water was the Word, and I saw churches as reservoirs, filling up with water, getting ready for Him to pull the switch. When God releases that *dunamis*, His power, out of our innermost being will flow "rivers of living water" (John 7:38), "for the earth shall be full of the knowledge of the Lord, as the waters cover the sea" (Isa. 11:9).

I transcribed this vision, and the man in whose home I was staying at the time took it to the Pacific Power Line Headquarters in Oregon. He asked to see the head engineer, and told him he would like to leave a paper for him to critique. My host said, "It is very important to us that we understand this material and know whether it is correct. The person who wrote it wants to know if it is accurate. If you would not mind taking some time to critique it, we will return for it in a few days." The engineer agreed to do so.

A few days later, my host returned to the Power Company. When he arrived, the receptionist told him the president of the company wanted to see him. She ushered him into the office of the president of the Pacific Power Company, who asked him, "Where did you get this information?" My host responded, "What would you say if I told you a little woman who cannot fix a light switch wrote it?" The president retorted, "I would say you are pulling my leg. This paper is one of the most scientific I have ever read. There are words and terms in here that only a few master electricians know and understand. Some of these terms are used only by the Pentagon. Whoever wrote this paper was a master electrician." My host then confessed, "I was wrong; forgive me. It wasn't the little lady who wrote it; she just copied it down. The Master Electrician— the Holy Spirit—described it to her."

The Greek word for "Holy Spirit" is *dunamis*, from which we derive our word "dynamo." The analogy of a power plant was a descriptive word picture to reveal the workings of our heavenly *Dunamis*.

My Father said to me, "I am running the pipes now." I heard the water roll in those pipes with my natural ear from October to December of that year. Finally I prayed, "Father, if it please You, turn the water sound inside, but let me continue to hear it." I have been to churches where I have heard the sound of those waters, confirming to me that they are reservoirs to be connected with the network of pipes. The Lord said to me, "This time when I pull that great power switch, no demon, devil, man or denomination will ever dam it up again, and many souls are going to be won. I will do a quick work; I am going to bring a revival that will reach the world."

In that vision, God let me see the ministry of the local church. I understood that we would take care of the elderly and feed the poor, train disciples and teach ministers, raising them up to possess the land. I saw the printed page rolling, and watched the Church walk into the heavenlies and take the powers of the media away from the devil. (After receiving this vision, I went through the country preaching what God had spoken to me, and people looked at me as if to say, "Poor thing, she is getting old.") I saw the grainfields of the world ready to be harvested, and my Father said it was going to happen soon. Since then I have stood on the shores of the isles of the sea in

Trinidad and the Bahamas and heard that water running. God gave me that vision over twenty-five years
ago, and I believe we are that much closer to fulfilling
our Father's dream.

PRE-REQUISITE FOR REVIVAL

There are conditions to be met if we expect to be
part of this coming revival. The power of the Holy
Spirit will only flow through those who have been
prepared to be His vessels. Much of what I had seen in
that vision related directly to the preparation of God's
people for the coming revival.

More recently, while I was waiting on God before
ministering on a Sunday to my congregation in Dallas,
Texas, my Father brought something to my attention
that shook me. My heart was tuned to what the Lord
wanted to say to the congregation that morning. As I
waited before the Lord, He spoke a word that dramatically influenced my leaving that pastorate, and has
shaped my preaching since that time. He said that
revival was not coming to America *unless* and *until* the
Church becomes more *personally* and *intimately acquainted* with the Third Part of the Godhead. We must
become more sensitive to Him and learn to cooperate
with Him, or revival will not come to this nation.
When He spoke of His Church, He wasn't talking
about an institution, a denomination or a building. He
was referring to the living organism, His Body, which
includes every person who has been born of His Spirit.

The Father deliberately referred to the Third Part of the Godhead, rather than the Holy Spirit, because He is intent in His purpose that we know the Holy Spirit as God.

"Father, are You saying the Charismatic church does not know the Third Part of the Godhead intimately, does not cooperate with Him and is not sensitive to Him?" I protested. I wept that night when He told me we are holding back the deluge of blessing that God intends us to have because we don't know the blessed Holy Spirit as we need to. With tears running down my cheeks, I cried, "My Father, ever since 1959, when You healed me and filled me with Your Holy Spirit, I have tried to walk in the Spirit. Please tell me what is wrong. What are you saying, Father, that I don't understand? Why don't we know this Third Person of the Godhead?"

The first reason He gave for our lack of relationship with the Holy Spirit was a *misinterpretation of the Scriptures.* That disturbed me, since I had spent seventeen years attempting to be an exegetical, systematic theology professor, rightly dividing the Word of God. He could not have spoken a more serious indictment to me than that I was not interpreting His Word correctly. However, He directed my attention to John, "Howbeit when he, the Spirit of truth, is come, he will guide you into all truth: for he shall not speak of himself; but whatsoever he shall hear, that shall he speak: and he will shew you things to come" (John 16:13). Then He showed me that the Church has taken the little preposition "of," in the phrase, "he does not speak *of* himself," and has taken it to mean that He does not speak *about* Himself. I had to admit that I have interpreted this Scripture in that way.

The Father asked me, "Why do you like to read the red letters in your Bible?" I replied, "Because they are the words of my Lord." He reminded me that Jesus did not say they were His words. Jesus said ". . . and the word which ye hear is not mine, but the Father's which sent me" (John 14:24b). Jesus spoke what He heard His Father speaking. When Jesus said of Himself, "I am the Way, the Truth, and the Life," He was teaching us about Himself, though the Source of revelation was the Father. In the same way, the Holy Spirit speaks about Himself, for the Scriptures tell us that the Holy Spirit wrote the Book. "For the prophecy came not in old time by the will of man: but holy men of God spake as they were moved by the Holy Ghost" (II Pet. 1:21). Since the Holy Spirit wrote the Scriptures, and there are over two hundred verses in the New Testament that tell us who He is, we must understand that the Holy Spirit speaks about Himself.

What, then, did Jesus mean when He said that the Holy Spirit will not speak *of* Himself? He meant that the Holy Spirit didn't speak *out of His own resources,* but was speaking what the Father gave Him to speak, just as Jesus did. The Father made me to understand that what we have taught in the Church about the Holy Spirit has given the impression that we should not inquire to know Him as a Person. We have taught that He doesn't speak about Himself because of His humility, and that His task is only to reveal Jesus to us. So we refer to the Holy Spirit as "it" or "tongues" or "gifts." Every Bible school I know of that includes a class on pneumatology studies "spiritual gifts" rather than the Person of the Holy Ghost. We have studied His gifts, not His Person. He is the Third Part of God; we need to become acquainted with Him personally.

The second reason we don't know the Holy Spirit intimately is that we don't have a *point of reference* for relating to Him. We understand the idea of a heavenly Father rather easily because of our relationships with our earthly fathers. I can say "Father," and relate to God somewhat as I related to my own daddy. My papa was perhaps the godliest person I have ever known, a man of sterling character. I am a minister of the Lord because my daddy taught me to love and obey him. Though I didn't always want to obey, my daddy didn't excuse my disobedience by saying, "She is just a child." He taught me that his word was to be obeyed and set up specific guidelines for me. I had no problems if I obeyed them, but if I didn't I would suffer the consequences. I learned that my daddy meant exactly what he said, which gave me a good understanding of how to respond to God's commands. My father was not just a

man of his word, however. He was also my dearest
friend in whom I could confide when I couldn't go to
anyone else.

When relating to my heavenly Father, I can simply
enlarge upon my understanding of my earthly father.
I don't have any problem crawling up in my heavenly
Father's lap and saying, "Put your arms around me,
Daddy, your daughter would like to talk to You." When
I don't understand something I just say, "Father, I
don't understand that. Will You talk to me about it?" I
expect Him to talk to me because of the way my daddy
talked to me. I believed what my daddy said. If there
is one thing on earth that my daddy would never have
done, it was to tell me a lie. For that reason, I can easily go to my heavenly Father and know that He is
truthful. So the night my heavenly Father called me
into the ministry, I did not consider disobeying my
"Daddy." Though I had never seen a female preacher, I
believed God when He told me He wanted me to
preach. And when my Father talks to me about what
is going to take place in the days ahead, I believe it
with all my heart, and am preparing for it. In this way,
our relationship to our earthly father becomes a point
of reference for helping us to relate to a heavenly
Father.

When we think of Jesus, the Son of God, we are
able to imagine the kind of person He was when He
walked the streets of Jerusalem. Each of us has an
image in our mind of Jesus when He was on earth. He

was limited to a human body that probably weighed less than 200 pounds and was less than six feet tall. He never traveled over 20 miles in one day, never wrote a book, never preached on radio or TV. He blessed children and healed the sick. His church consisted of twelve members, and one of them became a traitor. As we describe Jesus' life on this earth, we confirm our point of reference to His Person.

However, when we think of the Holy Spirit, we don't have any point of reference to understand His Person. He is a Person, just as the Father and the Son are Persons. He has taken up His residence in the Church, which is the body of Christ. Each of us is a temple of the Holy Spirit. We can see the beauty of God in each other because the Holy Spirit lives in us. When I see faces shining, I know the Holy Spirit is in those lives. His glory is in the Temple. Although this reality is somewhat abstract for us to grasp, we can learn to appreciate the beauty of God in our brothers and sisters as we see the Holy Spirit in their lives.

A third reason we do not know the Holy Spirit as a Person is that, because we have difficulty with corporeality, that which is not physical, we try to relate to Him through the *emblems* that represent Him and through *gifts* He bestows. We substitute fourteen emblems to represent Him, and say that they are the Holy Spirit. For example, we say the Holy Spirit is "the wind." He is not the wind, though He manifests

Himself in that way sometimes. Similarly, we call Him a dove. He has never been a dove, though He has used doves to manifest His Presence. Sometimes we refer to the oil of the Spirit, but the Holy Spirit is not oil. He is a Person, the Third part of the Godhead. During the Charismatic Movement we gave much of our attention to the gifts of the Holy Spirit. The Father sent the Holy Spirit to the Church with twenty-one gifts to help us on our homeward journey. However, we see His gifts and call them the Holy Spirit. Abraham sent his servant with gifts to find a wife for Isaac. The gifts were only to help them talk about Isaac until she arrived at her new home. The servant, representing the Holy Spirit in type, became her companion on the long journey home to find her bridegroom. The closer to her new home Rebekah came, the less she noticed gifts, and the more she looked for Isaac. When she saw him vaguely in sight, she asked if it was Isaac in the shadows and the servant told her it was. She was no longer involved in gifts, but was putting on a veil to get ready for the wedding. She had found her way to her bridegroom, not because of gifts she had received, but because of the servant companion who had led her home.

I understood then that, because of a misinterpretation of Scripture, we have de-emphasized the Holy Spirit's place as God. And because of our difficulty within corporeality, in that we have no point of reference, along with an over-emphasis on spiritual gifts, we have not given due regard to knowing the Third part of God as a Person. Some have stooped, and I feel it is an abomination, to refer to the Holy Spirit as "it." We need to respect Him as the third Person of God, who dwells in every believer. "Know ye not that your body is the temple of the Holy Ghost which is in you . . .?" (I Cor. 6:19) He is the Third Person of God who lives in the hearts of born-again believers, His Church.

WHAT IS A PERSON?

What constitutes a person? Inside each of us there is an inner sanctuary called our *spirit*. The human spirit is a vacuum, created in a shape that only the residence of the Almighty God can fill. No other person is able to fulfill the need of our spirits, for we were created for God's Presence. Surrounding that spirit, there is a soul which consists of our will or volition, our minds and our emotions. Our spirit and our soul are contained in our physical *body*, which makes every person a triune being made up of spirit, soul and body.

When we think of the Holy Spirit as a Person, we must understand that He has a will, He has a mind and He has emotions. We are to become His body to express the will of God in the Church. "And he who searches our hearts knows the mind of the Spirit, because the Spirit intercedes for the saints in accordance with God's will" (Rom. 8:27). The Holy Spirit acts in harmony with the *will* of God, praying through us according to His will. He knows the *mind* of God and wants to communicate that understanding to us so that our thoughts can become His thoughts. He also expresses emotion as a Person. Some people do not like His emotions. I once dared to tell Him I didn't believe in the emotion Pentecostals expressed in their worship. Even after I became one of them, I still wanted to eliminate the percussion, guitars, banjos and saxophone from the orchestra in my church, to make sure everything was done "decently and in order." Then one day the Holy Spirit asked me, "Whose order are you interested in, yours or Mine?"

After we began to experience worship in our church, my worship leader "disrupted" a service one night when I was out of town preaching. I arrived home the following day, and was greeted by a member of my church. "Pastor, you should have been home last night. We had a ball! We celebrated, worshiped and danced. They even pushed back the first row of chairs to make more room to dance." "They did what? Who did that?" I remonstrated. "The worship leader," was the joyous reply. I couldn't believe what I was hearing. "And you people got out on the floor and danced?" "Yes, Pastor, you would have loved it."

I was dying inside. Arriving at my office, I immediately sent for my worship leader, tactfully, graciously, and proceeded to advise him with my "wisdom." I said, "We don't believe in dancing. We believe in things being done scripturally and orderly." As I thought over this event later, still declaring I didn't believe in it, I heard another Voice inside me saying, "I know you don't, but I do." So I searched the Book to prove that it is not "lawful" to clap your hands or dance in church. Of course, I found that the Scriptures supported such expressions of worship. I didn't feel comfortable with this display of emotion, but I liked the Presence of God that it brought. Finally I realized my emotions were not His emotions, and that I needed to change.

So now I can dance, I can celebrate and shout, because I read in the Book, "Give a loud shout" (Ps. 65:13). We changed our orchestra so that before I left Fountain Gate, we had bass guitars and played tambourines, of all things. Worse than that, we rang bells. Everything that had breath, and that which didn't have breath, was praising God. The Holy Spirit has emotions that He wants to express through His people in praise, celebration, worship and prayer. He is a Person Who desires to dwell in believers, giving them the mind of God, doing the will of God and expressing godly emotions.

As we yield to the work of the Holy Spirit within us, we are cultivating a relationship with Him that will allow us to be part of fulfilling God's dream for a family that bears His Image. We learn to become more sensitive to His will and purposes and to cooperate with Him in His task of preparing a family for the Father.

The Third Person of God wants to indwell believers in a way that will bring us into perfect harmony with the purposes of God for our individual lives, our homes and our churches.

3

The Cultivation of God's Dream

The Holy Spirit Within Us

Cultivating a relationship with the Holy Spirit requires yielding to Him at every point where our wills, our thoughts and our desires differ with His divine purpose. The Holy Spirit comes to dwell in our spirits, filling us with the life of God. He must express that life, however, through our souls. God's will must become my will, His thoughts my thoughts and His desires my desires expressed through my volition, my mind and my emotions.

In Moses' Tabernacle, there was a veil between the Holy of Holies and the Holy Place that hid the presence of God from the view of the people. Only the high priest could go behind that veil, and he only once a year, to atone for the sins of the people. Scripture teaches that, as Christians, we are tabernacles of God. The presence of God dwells in the spirits of born-again believers. Most of us have Jesus "locked up" behind a veil in our spirits. I treated Him that way for seventeen years as an old-fashioned, holiness, Methodist preacher. Jesus was locked in my spirit, just as He was hidden from view behind the veil in Moses' Tabernacle.

I didn't know that I had Jesus locked behind the veil inside. I shouted joyfully when I understood that the veil of the Temple that had separated man from God's presence was rent asunder that day at Calvary. I rejoiced because the opening of that veil signified that I personally could go into God's presence. However, I did not realize that the veil of flesh in my soul kept the Spirit of God from filling my temple. When God sent the Holy Spirit to earth to dwell in our spirits and make us His temples, He planned to rip open that veil of flesh and allow Jesus to fill our entire sanctuary. His intent was to make our minds become His mind, our wills His will, our emotions His emotions. The Holy Spirit would fill each of our temples with His glory. This glory is not an essence to be seen floating in the shape of a cloud, but is rather the presence of God manifest in our lives and filling the Church.

When we ask the Person of the Holy Spirit to take His abode inside us, we surrender our all to Him. That being the case, I have a few questions to ask. Can you articulate what He has taught you this week? He is the Teacher. Do you know what the offices of the Holy Spirit are? How many of them has He fulfilled in you this week? Do you know His voice? Do you recognize His classroom? Did you ever ask Him why He came or what His mandate is?[1] He can't fulfill His mandate without dwelling in us, yet the people in whom He lives generally know very little about Him. We tell the Holy Ghost that our lives are His home. When He comes into our lives and finds things foreign to Him, He follows His mandate to clean us, change us and fill us full of the Godhead. He comes to teach us because He knows we are ignorant. He comes to clean us because He knows we are dirty. He comes to give us life because He knows we are dead. This is the only way we are ever going to be changed into the image of our Father. The Holy Spirit makes the Bible come alive, places that life inside us and changes our natures, replacing Adam's fallen nature with Christ's divine nature.

The Holy Spirit will often bring something to our attention and ask, "Is this yours?" Do we look at it and say, "No, it is my husband's"? Do we excuse ourselves by saying we got it from mama, or that we are a victim of child abuse? It seems everyone is a victim of something now. In reality, we are all victims of sin. We don't need to be petted and pampered, or justified for who we are. We need to be forgiven. Then we must allow

God to heal us, free us and change us into His image through our yielding to the Holy Spirit daily.

One of the ways we yield to the Holy Spirit is to praise and worship God. In the Scriptures, when we get a glimpse of life in heaven, we always see worship happening around the throne of God. The Holy Spirit enters the sanctuary of our spirits and sets our lives in harmony with the throne of God through worship.

Another way we yield to the Holy Spirit is by allowing Him to pray through us. There is a clearer teaching about prayer coming to the Church now. We are learning not to bring our want lists to the Father because we don't know what we need. There is Someone else in us Who prays according to the will of God for us. As Paul declared, "Likewise the Spirit also helpeth our infirmities: for we know not what we should pray for as we ought: but the Spirit itself maketh intercession for us with groanings which cannot be uttered. And he that searcheth the hearts knoweth what is the mind of the Spirit, because he maketh intercession for the saints according to the will of God" (Rom. 8:26-27).

If we don't experience His intercessions, we cannot claim the next verse, that promises, "And we know that all things work together for good to them that love God, to them who are the called according to his purpose" (Rom. 8:28). The Godhead is working out the Father's dream in our hearts. The Holy Spirit prays according to what is in the Father's heart, because He was in on the covenant before the foundation of the world. All things work together for good to those who love God and are called according to His eternal plan, His purpose. Because we don't know what is in the Father's heart, we don't know how to pray as we ought; but the Teacher does. So He comes to teach us to pray according to His will, which is ultimately to make us like Christ. "For whom he did foreknow, he also did predestinate to be conformed to the image of his Son, that he might be the firstborn among many brethren" (Rom. 8:29). Allowing the Holy Spirit to pray through us is an important part of our being conformed to His image.

Besides yielding to the Holy Spirit in praise and worship and allowing Him to pray through us, we must also allow Him to cleanse us in order that we might bear the family spirit in the image of God. It is here, perhaps, that we fail in our cooperation with the Holy Spirit. We do not develop sensitivity to Him, for we resist His convicting power that points to our need for change. We delight in His speaking in His languages and bringing gifts and power. But we don't want Him to go farther, because we find in the Book that when He comes, He brings with Him a broom, a fan, a fire and fuller's soap. He is expecting to clean up something that is dirty. Adam, with his self-life, has lived there and been in control long enough.

Now we have given the control of our lives to the Holy Spirit, though we know very little about Him. He

came to change our natures and to unveil the nature of
Jesus in us. Though He speaks in heavenly languages
and gives gifts, that is not the reason He came. His
mandate is to unveil the Christ who lives in us until
we know Him intimately as our Bridegroom and
reflect His image in our lives. His purpose is to bring
life to the written Word until it becomes the living
Christ to us, living His life through us.

Paul declares that it is "Christ in you, the hope of
glory" (Col. 1:27). One day Christ will fill our temples
with His glory. No one can make that happen except
the Holy Spirit. He came to split the veil of flesh open
and let Christ out of our spirits to fill our minds, our
wills and our emotions, and to quicken our mortal
bodies as well (Rom. 8:11).

This understanding of "Christ in you" does not deny
the reality of the literal Person of Jesus. Jesus is our
High Priest who "ever liveth to make intercession for
[us]" (Heb. 7:25). He invited Thomas to feel the scars
of His hands and side. Those scars are still there, and
that body now appears in the presence of God for us
(Heb. 9:24). We are looking for Jesus to appear again,
so that our decaying bodies can be changed and
fashioned like unto that body of glory (Phil. 3:21). That
is the hope of the Church. However, the work of the
Holy Spirit is to reveal the nature of Jesus in us. I was
not born with the mind of God, the will of God or the
emotions of God. My soul was warped. So when the

Holy Ghost moved into my spirit, He wanted to possess my temple.

As long as we are in control, He can't be. The "I" nature wants to rule, having my way and exercising my rights, never allowing the Holy Spirit to do what He came to do. If we take our "I" to the cross, we can exchange it there for the I AM. Then the Holy Spirit moves into every area of our personality, and the veil of flesh begins to fall away. We begin to realize that we don't think as we used to think. The truth will dawn on us: "These aren't my thoughts." Then we understand Paul's injunction to "Let this mind be in you, which was also in Christ Jesus" (Phil. 2:5). He also admonishes, "Whatsoever things are true, whatsoever things are honest, whatsoever things are just, whatsoever things are pure, whatsoever things are lovely, whatsoever things are of good report . . . think on these things" (Phil. 4:8).

The Holy Spirit begins to replace Adam's carnal mind with the mind of Christ so we can think like our Daddy thinks. Then He changes our rebellious wills as well. As we keep surrendering to the Holy Spirit, He begins to take the Father's will, that we know nothing about, and move into our wills. He makes our wills His will and His will our will. We don't have to pray in fear, wondering if we are doing what He wants. As we yield to the Holy Spirit's work within us, we begin to walk with God and to become the will of God.

In the same way, our emotions need to be changed by the Holy Spirit. Some of us may declare, "I am not emotional." God says, "I know, that is why I have to 'work you over.'" Our emotions constitute one third of our soul. If we do not express His emotions, that area of our personality is dead. When the Holy Spirit moves into our temples, He comes to set our houses in order, not just for eternity, but so we can live now as well. Then we can say with Paul, "I am crucified with Christ: nevertheless I live; yet not I, but Christ liveth in me: and the life which I now live in the flesh I live by the faith of the Son of God, who loved me, and gave himself for me" (Gal. 2:20).

A TESTIMONY

No doubt I would be dead today, were it not for a little preacher who had yielded himself to the Holy Spirit. He had learned to be sensitive to Him and to cooperate with Him. We had already had six deaths in our family, including those of my two brothers and my father. Just a few months earlier, an ambulance had carried me from a hospital in Greensboro, North Carolina, to my daddy's funeral. The nurses packed me carefully onto a stretcher so that my backbone would not vibrate, causing it to break into pieces. It seemed I was to be the next to join those of my family who had preceded me in death. I had resigned from my pastorate and from the college where I had taught, had chosen my pallbearers, and had listened to the trumpeter who was to play at my funeral.

At the cemetery where my daddy was being buried, I asked the undertaker not to lower his casket into the hole until I left. We had buried five other members of my family, and I had heard "ashes to ashes" all I wanted to hear it. So I asked them to leave him on the green mound. As my ambulance pulled away from that cemetery, I waved back at that green mound and said, "I will join you, Daddy, in a few months."

A few weeks earlier, when my father was ill, he had come walking out of his room with his Bible in his hand. He said to me, "Pastor, I think we have missed something" (I had been his pastor for nine years). I replied, "What have we missed, Papa?" He said, "I think we have missed knowing the God of Elijah. Elijah could lay his body on people and they were healed." With tears in his eyes, he asked, "Why is our family dying?" I told him what I had been taught. I said, "Daddy, we don't need that now. Healing is not for us today. That which is perfect has come. We have the Word. The Word is that which is perfect." As he left the room, he said to me, "I still believe the God of Elijah is alive." That was my last conversation with my father about the Word before His death.

A few months after my daddy's death, during which time I was admitted to two different North Carolina hospitals, I was carried into a church on a Sunday morning, one I had not been in before. I was expecting that service to perhaps be the last I would ever attend.

The man who was to preach was not the pastor of the church. He was the former pastor who was now a superintendent, but had been invited to speak that particular Sunday. He was over seventy years old, and he knew God. *He knew the Holy Spirit.* He arrived on Saturday and was staying in a hotel, preparing to speak the following morning.

At four o'clock on Sunday morning, the Holy Spirit awakened him and instructed him to preach a sermon entitled, "Where Is the Lord God of Elijah?" He reminded the Lord that he had already preached that sermon to this church when he was pastoring there. The Lord replied, "I know that, I keep the records." God simply requested him to preach what He asked him to preach. In obedience to the Spirit of God he preached about the God of Elijah, not knowing I would be present in that congregation. He could not have known of the conversation about Elijah that I had with my daddy. He simply followed the mind of the Spirit and set the stage for what caught my attention, the "Faith of Elijah." If he had spoken on healing, I would have turned him off. If he had preached about speaking in tongues, I would not have been listening. As a Methodist professor, my theology would not have accepted it. I was a born-again, prayed up, paid up, packed up woman ready to go up, but I didn't believe in healing or speaking in tongues.

That little man did one of the most unusual things I had ever seen. As he was preaching, he declared, "If you had the faith of Elijah, you could see what Elijah saw." Then he stepped beside the pulpit, looked me straight in the eye, and said, "My beloved, you may have followed behind the dearest one on earth to you and left him on a *green mound*, but he wants you to know that he did not take his God away from you. The God of Elijah is in this church today."

At that moment, the God of Elijah nudged me to go forward for prayer. I responded, "They are not having an altar call." In a few moments we began to sing an old Methodist hymn. The words of the third stanza were, "He saw me plunged in deep distress, and He flew to my release." When we began singing those words, the Holy Spirit spoke to me again, telling me to go forward for prayer. I asked the lady who had brought me to the church to stand me up. Thinking I was suffering, she responded, "We will be leaving in a few minutes." I repeated, "Stand me up." Later, she told me that the tone of my voice let her know she had better stand me up, which she hastened to do.

In the eyes of all those people, I did something that ordinarily would have made me feel totally out of order. I walked up, looked into that preacher's face and said, "Sir, I don't know why I am here. In obedience to God's prompting I have come. Maybe you should pray for me." He reached into the podium and brought out a vial of oil and "greased" me. After praying a simple prayer, he said, "In Jesus' Name," in a way I had never heard it said before. I knew that man knew Him in a way I did not.

I thanked him and started dragging myself back to my seat in my braces. What crossed my mind was that I must have been anointed for my burial. When I reached the seventh row, where I had been sitting, God spoke to me in a thundering voice. I thought everyone in the church heard it. He said, "If ye be willing and obedient, ye shall eat the good of the land" (Isa. 1:19). Standing there in my braces, I suddenly knew I was going to live, though I thought I would remain crippled. God asked me if I was willing to be identified with these Pentecostal people. I said, "Yes, Sir."

Turning in my braces, I said to the preacher, "Sir, may I give a testimony?" He replied that testimonies were in order there. Hugging my Bible, with tears running down my cheeks, I said to that church, "Jesus has just told me I am going to live. I believe I am going to get to preach this Book yet." Even crippled for the rest of my life, it would be wonderful to live to preach the Word. When I had finished saying that and started into my seat, the power of God struck the base of my cranium. It traveled down my spine and came back up to my head. One hour and twenty minutes later, I had danced all over that church, right out of my braces, run the aisle, and exhausted every adjective I could find to thank God for healing my body! (They told me later there were three hundred people on the floor acting as "bad" as I was acting.)

I shouted, "Bless the Lord, O my soul, and all that is within me!" My soul obeyed me, and I heard a new language come out of my mouth, one that I didn't understand or believe in. I listened to the Electrician of Eternity pick up the phone, dial heaven and say, "Give heaven this new address of an earthly temple. I have just moved in to set up worship and communion inside her, and to cleanse this temple. I will set up My classroom and write the Word of God on the tablets of her heart." The Holy Spirit had invaded a Methodist minister's sanctuary. I spent the next five years trying to find out Who this Third Part of God was. I searched the Scriptures to learn about the One Whom I had thought I already knew.

THE HOLY SPIRIT IN THE CHURCH

I was grieved when God told me that the Church doesn't know the Holy Spirit as we need to. I wept that night, vowing by the grace of God to do all I could to help people come to know the Holy Spirit. He came to set up the spirit of supplication and grace, of resurrection and life. He operates in seven different moods and manifests seven different powers through us. He is assigned sixty-six different functions in every one of us.[1] When we cooperate with Him, we become people who walk in the Spirit. Paul prayed for the church at Ephesus, "That the God of our Lord Jesus Christ, the

Father of glory, may give unto you the spirit of wisdom
and revelation in the knowledge of him: The eyes of
your understanding being enlightened; that ye may
know what is the hope of his calling, and what the
riches of the glory of his inheritance in the saints"
(Eph. 1:17-18). I had always thought that Paul prayed
for the church at Ephesus, that they would have the
spirit of wisdom. However, the Holy Spirit prayed
through Paul for the entire Church, and His prayers
will be answered. The Church is going to have the
spirit of wisdom to know Who Jesus is. What is ahead
is not just a little word of wisdom once in a while. The
spirit of wisdom will settle on the Church and open
our spiritual eyes and ears until we can see and hear
the truth of the Word of God.

We are going to be changed into His image and become the family of God by yielding to the work of the
Holy Spirit in us. The Holy Spirit came to give us the
family spirit, because we don't have anything akin to
it. The family spirit is the Lamb spirit, the spirit of a
servant. The very nature of the Third Person of God is
the nature of a Servant, doing the Father's bidding to
give to us the life of Jesus and to present a family to
the Father. As we come to know the Holy Spirit personally, we will undoubtedly find ourselves yielding to
the call to servanthood.

NOTES

1. Dr. Pickett has a complete study of the Holy Spirit available in outline form. Write to Dr. Fuchsia Pickett, 394 Glory Road, Blountville, TN 37617.

4

The Call of God's Dream

The Servant Spirit

Those who understand what God is saying today are hearing the call of the Holy Spirit for the perfecting of His Church. Everywhere I travel, I find that those who are flowing in God's present moving are preaching these same themes which express God's heartcry for His Church today. This is an eight-fold cry of the heart of the Lord.

The first of those themes is *repentance*. Repentance must become a continuous process in our walk with God, rather than something we do one time when we receive Jesus as Savior. It is necessary that repentance become a way of life for us so that we experience the holiness God requires. A second theme to which God is calling His Church is true *holiness*, which is our nature exchanged for God's nature. He is making us holy because He is holy, and He is going to have a holy Church. God has also declared that His house shall be a house of prayer for all nations (Isa. 56:7). He is calling His Church to *prayer*. *Revival* is another of God's calls to His Church today. He is beginning even now to move in many churches in a way that can only be identified as a cleansing move of God. It is just beginning, but many are testifying of Holy Ghost revival in their churches.

God's purposes include full *restoration* of the Church and of the home to divine order. Unfortunately, the Church world has taken the doctrine of fallen man and taught it as "divine order." God's intention, however, is to restore the home to His divine order. *Forgiveness* must flow as well between brothers and sisters in the Church to fulfill God's purposes. In her most recent book, *The Forgiving Church*, Sue Curran writes: "Our churches maintain their vitality through the cleansing and release of forgiveness. The disease of unforgiveness threatens that life, for where the church fails to forgive it ceases to live."[1] The call to *worship* God in spirit and in truth is ringing loud and clear today. I believe God is calling the Church to a higher dimension of worship than she has experienced before. All these themes are timely messages of the Spirit of God to the Church today, offering truth that can set us free to fulfill God's dream for a family that bears His image.

However, we are not hearing very much about one of the key calls of God to the Church, without which it will be impossible to fulfill God's dream. For God to realize His dream for a family, His children must respond to the call to *servanthood*—to becoming a servant. It is quite possible that our definition of success differs dramatically from God's idea of true greatness. Jesus told His disciples ". . .whosoever will be great among you, let him be your minister; and whosoever will be chief among you, let him be your servant" (Matt. 20:26-27). We must learn to value what God values and esteem what He esteems. Perhaps the truth of servanthood is not an exciting revelation; but without allowing it to become a reality in our lives, we cannot hope to become part of fulfilling God's dream. Jesus came not to be served, but to serve (Matt. 20:28), and Scripture portrays the Holy Spirit as a servant also. Our attitude is to be the same as that of Jesus "Who . . . made Himself nothing, taking the very nature of a servant" (Phil. 2:7, NIV).

SERVANT BY CHOICE

The apostle Paul declared, "For though I be free from all men, yet have I made myself servant unto all, that I might gain the more" (I Cor. 9:19). What Paul actually said was that he made himself a slave to serve everyone in order to bring them to an understanding of the gospel. What was Paul's perspective of servanthood? He was a Hebrew who was well acquainted with the law. He knew that during the time of the Old Testament, slaves were freed every seventh year. When a slave was freed, he could choose to stay with his master. He would not be a bond slave any longer, but would become a love slave. If he chose to do that, he declared it publicly by laying his head on the doorpost and allowing someone to bore a hole in his ear. By placing an earring in his bored ear, he declared he was no longer a bond-slave, but was by choice love slave for the rest of his life (Exod. 21:1-6).

For a long time I voiced a prayer and didn't really know what I was asking. I prayed, "Father, open my ears, and let me be where I can hear You." As I was studying the Word, I learned that to have your ear "digged" or opened means to have it "bored." The psalmist cried, "My ear hast thou opened . . ." (Ps. 40:6) The opening of our ear to hear God's voice requires the process of having it bored, as was the ear of the love slave. We should not wonder why we cannot hear what God is saying to the Church if we have not had our ear bored and become a love slave. That involves coming to the Father and declaring, "I am not serving You for promotion or position; I'm not serving You for pay or for profit, vacation or benefits. I'm serving You because I love the family spirit. I choose to be a love slave." When we say that we do not hear God speak to us, we are making an announcement affirming that we are not servants. A *doulos* is a love slave with a bored ear who, without hesitation, reservation or further information, does what the Master says. There is nothing in the love slave that wants to refuse. He never expects to choose another profession or seek another master. He serves because of love and because he wants to represent his master. This servant's only concern is that he recognize the Master's voice. Jesus said, "My sheep hear my voice" (John 10:27).

THE MASTER'S CALL

God is faithful to speak to us about our responsibilities in our relationship to Him and His promise of provision in His relationship to us. He has carefully clarified our "job description" as servants to let us know what He expects of us. As we fulfill the Scriptures regarding the call to servanthood, we can know we are pleasing Him and finding His favor.

One of the first things we must understand is that we are not co-chairmen, but *co-laborers with God*. The Scriptures declare that "We are labourers together with God" (I Cor. 3:9). God is the unquestionable Chief from Whom we receive all our instructions. Jesus challenges us to "Take my yoke upon you, and learn of me" (Matt. 11:29). He is telling us to learn of His nature, for He is gentle and lowly of heart. Then we shall find rest for our souls, for His yoke is easy and His burden is light. To be a yokefellow simply means to work together as a teammate. Servanthood is the path of peace for all who will truly follow Christ.

As we choose to become co-laborers with God in the path of servanthood, the Lord teaches us where our *source of strength* for service lies. "They that wait upon the Lord shall renew their strength" (Isa. 40:31). We know there is a waiting on God in prayer to receive His empowering. However, the word "wait" used in this verse is the same word as used in the phrase "waiting on tables": serving. Servants get tired. "They that wait upon the Lord shall renew their strength . . . they shall run, and not be weary; and they shall walk, and not faint" (Isa. 40:31). As we take the attitude of servants in our work for the Lord, He will renew our strength.

Paul wrote to the Corinthians ". . . our sufficiency is of God" (II Cor. 3:5). A servant is always dependent on his master, never self-sufficient. We will soon run out of strength if we try to be sufficient in ourselves. God must become our sufficiency as we learn to depend on Him. The Greek word for sufficiency means "a warehouse with no back wall to it." When we get inside that warehouse, we start shouting about the "unsearchable riches of Christ . . . the height, the breadth, the length . . ." as Paul did. We can never exhaust God's sufficiency. However, we won't have a key to the warehouse without first having a servant spirit. As servants we are co-laborers with God, and He becomes our sufficiency for service.

The Scriptures also give promise of status to the one who has a true servant's heart. "He that waiteth on his master *shall be honoured*" (Prov. 27:18). God esteems His servants and considers them to be worthy of honor. I have been privileged to meet many of God's servants as I travel in ministry. Standing in a church in Georgia, I observed a pastor, a humble little woman, who is spiritual dynamite. If anyone has taught a church to love Jesus, it is this woman. I have never seen a congregation so in love with Jesus. This pastor is in love with Him, absolutely love-sick. She had visited many camps and seminars, searching for truth, but couldn't be satisfied that she was hearing what the Lord was saying to the Church in this hour. She returned to her church and wept. Sick of hearing about methods and programs, she decided to stay home until God sent her "help from the sanctuary." During that time, the Lord sent me to minister in her church. After I ministered the Word, that pastor stood with her church, shouting and praising the Lord. I didn't know why they were shouting. Someone said to me, "God has answered our pastor's prayers to be able to hear the word of the Lord." While I was there, she made one of the most profound statements I have ever heard. "I was crying out for God to send help from the sanctuary," she said. "He told me that if we would honor those whom He sent to us, He would send us those whom He honored." God honors His servants. Jesus said ". . . if any man serve me, him will my Father honour" (John 12:26).

I had an interesting experience in my pastorate when the Holy Spirit chose to honor a servant. We

graduated eleven high school seniors one year from
the academy at Fountain Gate Ministries, and nine of
them enrolled in our Bible College. When we prepared
to lay hands on them and pray for them in our Sunday
morning service, the Holy Spirit said to me, "Honor
where honor is due." I asked Him where it was due,
and He spoke the name of the teacher who had left her
mark on these students during the first six years of
their lives. So instead of calling the elders of the
church first, I asked Jeri Decker to come forward. I
said to her, "These are your children. You get to usher
them into Bible College." When these young people
were very small, I had heard her say, "If I am to leave
a print in the cement of their lives to shape them, I
must step into them while the cement is still wet."
That was an expression of her servant heart. God
Himself will honor those who serve with a true
servant's heart.

A SERVANT'S HEART

A servant is not someone who does something with
gritted teeth or has left skid marks along the way in
following Jesus. He is not someone who does a certain
task because he is not qualified to do something
greater. Nor is he a person "put down" to a low status
because of race, creed or color. A servant is someone
who has *chosen* to reflect in his life the family image of
God.

In the life of Abigail, we see a woman who displayed
this family spirit. She had a very mean husband, a

man who was a drunkard (I Sam. 25:3-10). God judged him worthy of death for insulting David. As a result of her godly behavior, this precious wife received a message from King David; he wanted her to become his wife. David was the king, the prophet, the priest, the sweet singer of Israel. He honored Abigail by asking her to become his wife. If we had received such an invitation, we might have published it in the newspaper, called reporters and dress designers, and celebrated with parties. What an honor! When Abigail received the invitation, she bowed her face to the earth and showed her humility and submission, saying, "Behold, let thine handmaid be a servant . . ." (I Sam. 25:41) She was invited to become David's wife, yet her response to him was, "Let me be a servant to wash the feet of the servants of my lord" (v.41). She could have immediately taken on an air of superiority, but instead she chose to respond in a spirit of humility.

Servanthood is determined by who we *are*, not by what we *do*. True servanthood involves heart reality. We must learn to see ourselves and every other believer in relationship to the Lord Jesus Christ, rather than evaluating each other's worth by our positions or titles. Every person must be valued for who he is, rather than for what he does. What we do is a result of who we are. That understanding may be contrary to our idea of who a servant is. We consider a hireling, someone who does hourly work and performs a task we would rather not perform, to be a servant. If we call people servants because of what they do, our idea of a servant must change. Servanthood is determined by who we are. When we begin to see ourselves primarily as servants, it won't make any difference to us what we are asked to do. If we are to reflect the character of Jesus, we must develop a servant's heart. Can we humble ourselves as Jesus did? He emptied Himself in eternity, stripping Himself of all privilege and every title, humbling Himself by choice to become the obedient Servant to carry out His Father's wishes. Because He was willing to humble Himself, the Father has highly honored Him (Phil. 2:7).

Our place of authority with God, not just hereafter, but here on earth, will be determined by our having the attitude of a servant. When we know Who God is, we will choose to serve Him above everything else on earth. One of the most beautiful examples of a servant spirit I have ever seen is in the life of the pastor with whom I left my church in Texas. The outstanding characteristic that my husband and I saw in Dr. Sam Sasser during the seven years before we asked him to come and pastor our church was his attitude of a servant. He never sought to be honored or seen as special. Though he is highly educated, having four earned doctorate degrees, he always in honor prefers others before himself. He has a servant spirit and God has honored him by allowing him to minister in places where very few may go.

Our servant heart will be expressed in all our relationships. I love my husband, LeRoy Pickett. Everywhere he goes with me, people say to him, "This is 'Honey,' isn't it? We know you already." Pastors say to him, "That woman loves the ground you walk on." Do you think it is a chore for me to do something for him? A servant who is not a hireling doesn't always have to be told everything he has to do. He knows his master well enough to know what he wants and to do it. Some of us have secretaries who are true servants. My secretary anticipates me before I ever get to the task. She is not waiting for me to come and tell her what to do. Very often she will say to me, "I count it a privilege; I feel I have been honored to work with you." It is an honor to me to have her work for me. I am going to take good care of her, because I might not get another secretary like Judy. She is special. Servants are special. They are not hirelings or wage earners, but people who reflect the family spirit of God in their work and relationships.

THE GREATEST SERVANT

Becoming a servant means that, by our choice, we are "in honor preferring one another" (Rom. 12:10). Jesus preferred us above Himself, willingly suffering the supreme sacrifice of giving His life to redeem us. Paul admonished us to . . .

Let this mind be in you, which was also in Christ Jesus: Who, being in the form of God, thought it not robbery to be equal with God: but made himself of no reputation, and took upon him the form of a servant . . . (Phil. 2:5-7).

In the Garden of Gethsemane, Jesus revealed His servant heart when He prayed, "O my Father, if it be possible, let this cup pass from me: nevertheless not as I will, but as thou wilt" (Matt. 26:39). He did not pray this out of fear, as some teach. It is blasphemous to think there was cowardice in our Lord. Jesus knew He was the Lamb, "slain before the foundation of the world." He knew Who He was and that He came to die. He went to the garden as the Servant and the Lamb. Then why did He pray in that way? Is it possible that in that garden the Father revealed to Jesus that He would not only be the Lamb of God, but the Scapegoat as well? Once a year on the Day of Atonement the Israelites took ashes of the sin offering and put them on the head of the scapegoat. They would then send that goat outside the city wall, never to be retrieved. This they did to atone, in type, for the sin principle in man, that which causes him to transgress. That night in the garden, did God unveil to Jesus that not only would He fulfill the sacrifice of the Lamb, to take away the sins of the world, but that of the Scapegoat as well, to redeem man from the sin principle? Jesus knew that the scapegoat was never retrieved. Was He expressing in His agony that night, "Father, if there is no other way to save Your family, I will not only be the sacrificed Lamb, I will become the Scapegoat as well.

If there is no other way, I will go, never to come back"? He proved His explicit trust in the Father's will when He cried from the cross, "Father, into thy hands I commend my spirit" (Luke 23:46).

We see in the life of the servant Moses the willingness to have his name blotted out in order for God's people to be rescued. He prayed, "Yet now, if thou wilt forgive their sin—; and if not, blot me, I pray thee, out of thy book which thou hast written" (Exod. 32:32). And the apostle Paul declared that he could wish himself accursed and cut off from Christ for the sake of his brothers (Rom. 9:3). It is impossible that mere human ministers would experience a more sacrificial love for mankind than their Lord. Jesus became a willing Servant to accomplish our ultimate redemption, whatever the cost. Our two-fold redemption was fulfilled on Calvary, the sin principle destroyed. Paul declares to us in the Book of Romans: "For the law of the Spirit of life in Christ Jesus hath made me free from the law of sin and death" (Rom. 8:2).

Jesus became the greatest Servant of all by humbling Himself to become man and the servant of men, and then giving His life as the perfect sacrifice for mankind's redemption. On the eve of His death, during the last supper with His disciples, He gave us one more glimpse of the family spirit. *Knowing* that the Father had given all things into His hands, Jesus took a towel and girded Himself and washed His disciples' feet (John 13:4-5). After His resurrection from the dead, having won the supreme victory over sin, Jesus still revealed the humble servant spirit to His disciples the morning He cooked their breakfast on the shore of the lake. The disciples had gone fishing. "As soon as they were come to land, they saw a fire of coals there, and fish laid thereon, and bread. Jesus saith unto them . . . Come and dine" (John 21:9-12). That servant spirit is the nature of the family of God. Jesus never manifested any other spirit.

We call servanthood an unpopular doctrine because to embrace it requires death to our selfish natures, our desire to rule. In order for us to be changed into the likeness of Jesus, we must become servants. I didn't learn this truth in school. As seminary students, we dreamed of becoming great ministers or pastors. Our true call, however, is to be like Jesus, Who chose to become a servant. The greatest role to which we can aspire is to be changed into the likeness of Jesus and become servants. As we allow the Holy Spirit to work on our natures, we will reflect the character of Jesus in our lives. Our response to the call to servanthood determines whether we will be part of fulfilling God's dream.

NOTES

1.   Curran, Sue, *The Forgiving Church*, Shekinah Publishers, 1990, Blountville, TN, p. vii.

5

The Character of God's Dream

Response to Servanthood

Responding to the call to servanthood involves scrutinizing the attitudes and motivation which form the basis of our character. Solomon taught that, "As [a man] thinketh in his heart, so is he" (Prov. 23:7). If in our hearts we see ourselves as wonderful people with tremendous potential for becoming great in some sphere of life or ministry, we have not yet responded to the call to servanthood. When we see ourselves as blood-bought children of God, no longer belonging to ourselves, our response will be, "Lord, I love You enough to serve You." A true servant heart pursues *holiness* and *purity of motive* in service.

67

Sometimes people serve with mixed motives. If we are doing a task to receive recognition for it, we are not doing it with a servant spirit. Paul wrote to the Ephesians, "Slaves, obey your earthly masters with respect and fear, and with sincerity of heart just as you would obey Christ" (Eph. 6:5, NIV). God is looking for one who serves to please Christ. Some serve out of a desire to get "brownie points." My former staff used to tease each other about doing something special for Pastor. They would say, "Aha, you are trying to get brownie points to earn her favor." We serve God because we love Him, not to earn His favor.

Others serve because they are attempting to "work out their own salvation." We need to understand that we don't serve to get to heaven. That is still difficult for me to grasp because of my religious background. I somehow feel that if I can serve Him better, I can merit His favor. However, that is not how we merit His favor. We must be cleansed of this kind of thinking. We must not attend church because of what the pastor will think of us if we don't. We should not give our tithes because someone will see the record and know how we gave. We give because we love the One who gave us life, even if no one sees the record.

Our motivation for serving is as important as our service, for God is looking for servant hearts to reflect the spirit of the Lamb. As we allow the Holy Spirit to teach us to become part of the family of God, He will change our motivation and our attitudes to reflect the Lamb spirit. Paul taught us what the fruit of a Spirit-filled life would look like when he wrote, "But the fruit of the Spirit is love, joy, peace, longsuffering, gentleness, goodness, faith, meekness, temperance: against such there is no law" (Gal. 5:22-23).

A true servant will be motivated by love. I want to be able to sing as an elderly, gray-headed professor who taught me in college. He would come into our Pentateuch class and, without any formality of opening remarks, would bow his head, shake his gray hair, and sing, "He loves me, He loves me, He loves me this I know; He gave Himself to die for me, because He loves me so." We students would end up on the cement floor crying our eyes out because of the presence of God that filled the classroom. When he got through singing, we didn't think we knew God at all. He was the most brilliant man of the college, and the most humble. On work day, he was present. When there were leaves to be raked, he was there. They would say, "Dr. Burkholder, you don't need to do that." He would say, "Oh, but I do. I am doing it for Jesus." Everywhere he went he could be heard singing, "He loves me, He loves me."

If we serve the Lord selfishly for what He gives us, we would serve the devil if he paid higher wages. If our motivation for serving God is that He blesses and heals and prospers us, we are displaying the spirit of the hireling. Those who respond to the call to servant-hood serve Jesus because they love Him. When we love ourselves more than we love God, we are not willing to become servants. Love slaves have a supreme desire that the Master know they are serving because they love Him.

Joy is the desired attitude of a servant. "The joy of the Lord is our strength" (Neh. 8:10). According to Dr. David Schoch, that verse literally reads, "The joy we give God in serving Him gives us back His strength." God's genuine approval of our service becomes strength for us to serve. A servant does each task joy-fully. He doesn't stop working five minutes early, deciding not to start something else because it is quit-ting time. Neither is his attitude dependent upon his circumstances always being pleasant. It is written of Jesus, "Who for the joy that was set before him en-dured the cross . . ." (Heb. 12:2) Jesus' suffering did not destroy His joy. A servant can endure great dif-ficulty because he is convinced that his greatest privilege on earth is to serve God.

I loved my earthly daddy so much that it was a delight for me to serve him. I was delighted when he asked me to get his coffee, instead of asking my mother. When he asked me to make him some cornbread, do you think I felt it was belittling? I prac-ticed and practiced, dumping out one pan of cornbread after another until I could be sure I had made some that would please my daddy. It was my joy to serve him. If I could experience that joy in serving my earthly daddy, how much more should I rejoice in serving my heavenly Father? I am a daughter of God, and it is a supreme joy to serve Him. When we live as true servants, our service brings us pleasure; we don't complain over any menial task.

Faithfulness further characterizes the servant heart. A servant is a faithful steward, or overseer. A steward takes care of something that belongs to another person until that one can return to take care of it. As an overseer, he does not require the master to write out all the instructions, but is able to take responsibility within a certain latitude. A servant develops as he works in an area, exploring its needs and responding to them. Every Christian has been given stewardship of a treasure within, that is, the life of Jesus that God has invested in us. We are responsible to allow the character of Christ to be developed in us as we yield to the Holy Spirit's conviction and promptings, showing us where we need to be changed. We will not be rewarded for our educational degrees or our personal excellence, but for our faithful obedience as servants.

Our greatest commendation will be for God to say to us, "Well done, thou good and faithful servant . . ." (Matt. 25:21) He does not commend the "preacher," "apostle," or "minister," but the *servant*. If we earn

God's commendation we have truly succeeded in life, whether or not we have succeeded in man's eyes. I knew a man who gave a beautiful piano concert one evening. When he had finished, everyone in the auditorium stood to give an ovation, except for one man. The musician left the auditorium sadly with his head down. Someone later remarked to him about the wonderful ovation he had received; he replied that he didn't think it was wonderful. The friend reminded him that everyone in the auditorium had stood to congratulate him. The musician answered, "There was one who did not stand, and he was my *teacher*. I would rather he had stood than all the others." For the true servant of God, there is only One whose commendation we want to hear, and that is God's. If all the other people think we are wonderful, but we have not pleased our Father, we will have failed.

On the day I stand before the Master, I want to hear Him say, "Well done, good and faithful servant." I began praying to hear Him say that forty-one years ago, when He called me and said, "If you love Me, feed My sheep." We respond to the servant call by being willing to feed His sheep. However, sheep aren't always very nice. There are a lot of things we could do that would seem more worthwhile than feeding sheep. One night when I was praying and telling the Lord how much I loved Him, He said to me, "I know you love Me; you are feeding My sheep." Our measure of love is not found in how many gifts we have or how highly someone thinks of us. We evaluate our love by our faithfulness to obey what He has asked us to do.

Faithfulness results in our becoming addicted to service. In the New Testament we read of the house of Stephanus which had addicted themselves to ministry. The Greek reads, "They made up their minds to serve as servants; they were addicted" (I Cor. 16:15). When you are addicted to something, you feel as though you can't live without it. The house of Stephanus could not live without serving; they were addicted to it.

Shekinah Ministries of Blountville, Tennessee is a beautiful example of a church that is addicted to service. They host several ministers' conferences each year. My husband and I attended these conferences for ten years before moving there as a headquarters for our traveling ministry. We had never been to a place where people are willing to give up their best room, move their children out of their bedrooms, and do anything else that is needed to give ministers a place to stay during conferences. Their question is not, "Do we have an *extra* room?" but rather, "How can we vacate a room to make it available for the ministers?" My husband and I stayed in Judy Weatherford's home every year for eight years. We learned to just walk on in and put our things away, making ourselves at home. In every home of the congregation, people move out or over to serve the visiting ministers. They specialize in investing their lives in this ministry, devoting themselves to hospitality for Christian brothers. God will reward them for the faithfulness which has resulted in their addiction to service.

If joy is our attitude, and faithfulness our measure of love, we can describe *humility* as the demeanor of our servant heart. A proud spirit will rarely be joyful, nor will it be faithful to any task that does not satisfy its ego. A love slave is willing to keep a low profile, without needing a title for everything he does. He produces what the Father wants without exalting himself by using titles. I dislike the way some people refer to themselves as apostles or prophets. Although it is true that Paul referred to himself as an apostle, he also called himself a servant of the Lord. I would rather just *do* the ministry and let someone else decide what to call it. The spirit of our Father's family is not a spirit of exaltation or pride, but is exemplified in the spirit of the Lamb Who sacrificed Himself to redeem us. Humility characterizes those who are full of the Holy Spirit. The spirit of the family of God is the spirit of the prodigal son who has come to himself, is broken, and is anxious to come home to daddy, saying, "Make me as one of your servants" (Luke 15:19).

When I was practicing nursing in Eden, North Carolina, a precious man whom I had known from my childhood was admitted to the hospital as a patient. He was Dr. William Gordon, an Episcopal priest in our city. It would take a lot of space to tell you the things this man did in our little town that proved to everyone he was a man of God. I don't know anyone else who ever graced our city with the Spirit of Christ like this man did. He wore his vestments on Sunday; he stood in his pomp and said his prayers from his prayer book. But Monday night at midnight, when no one was looking, he would be down in the poor section of town. He could be seen picking up a coal scuttle to take someone some coal. The cobbler told me that many times Dr. Gordon would walk in with a little boy from the poor section of town and say, "Would you half-sole his shoes?" The cobbler looked at the priest's shoes and saw that there were larger holes in them than in the boy's.

When this priest became a patient in the hospital, the staff respected him so much they assigned the superintendent of nurses to give him his bath. She told me that as she bathed his feet, tears dripped down her cheeks because of the regard she had for him. When he died, stores closed, businesses sent flowers and government offices in Raleigh closed for the day to honor him. A servant of God had made his mark on our city. May God help us to leave the mark of one who picks up the towel and washes the feet of others. Humility is a beautiful attribute of the servant heart. Without humility there is no true servanthood. God is calling for servants who will be filled with the fruit of the Holy Spirit. He is not seeking those who desire honor and recognition, but those who serve Him because they love Him supremely.

A SERVANT'S GARMENT

We cannot respond to the call to servanthood without being secure in our identity as a person. Without knowing who we are in God, we will never choose to become servants. That is why the understanding of God's eternal plan for each of us is so important, for it gives meaning and purpose to our lives and sets us free to become servants of God. The greater the understanding we have of who we are, the less we feel we have to "prove" to ourselves and others. On the night of the last supper with His disciples, the Scripture says that "Jesus *knowing* that the Father had given all things into His hands, and that he was come from God, and went to God; He riseth from supper, and laid aside his garments; and took a towel, and girded himself. After that he poureth water into a basin, and began to wash the disciples' feet, and to wipe them with the towel wherewith he was girded" (John 13:3-5). Jesus knew Who He was and that everything in the world belonged to Him. With that knowledge, He rose from supper, took a towel, poured water into a basin, and began to wash the disciples' feet.

When we know who we are we can do as Jesus did. A strong sense of identity and a healthy self-esteem makes us willing to humble ourselves to become servants.

Because of self-conceit and pride, some Christians render themselves useless in the Kingdom. We have seen great churches and big ministries fall when leaders became exalted through pride. Only by humbling ourselves to become servants can we avoid falling to pride. The apostle Paul warned, "For I say, through the grace given unto me, to every man that is among you, not to think of himself more highly than he ought to think . . ." (Rom. 12:3)

It is important to realize that a servant's garment is fitted to size, tailor-made by God for each servant. No one else can wear yours. Once you get that robe on, it has the sweetest aroma of any garment you can wear, because servants go to the garden to pick spices for the king (Song of Sol. 1:12). We must also understand that the garment of a servant is not to be worn on certain occasions only, or in special situations. Some people will serve the pastor or officials in the church, but they won't willingly serve someone else for fear of not receiving any recognition for what they do. As we have seen, recognition is not the goal of the servant heart.

Another fact about the servant's garment is that we don't have to worry about putting it under lock and key. A servant's robe is never stolen. Though people may stand in line to get our positions, they will not do so to get our servant's robe. There are enough servants' garments for all who will humble themselves to respond to the call to servanthood. Servants don't have to make good impressions; they are known by the garment they wear.

A servant's garment carries with it a lovely aroma. There is nothing more fragrant than a *poured-out life.* Helen Vincent Washburn lived such a life. I was privileged to sit at her feet for four years. Besides being the greatest teacher I have ever heard, she was the most beautiful woman I have ever seen, with clear blue eyes, blond hair and fair complexion. She was the epitome of charm and grace and could mingle with the most highly cultured or the least cultured of this country without embarrassing anyone. The poor man would be as totally comfortable with her as would more prominent people.

Her teaching ministry made me hungry for the Word. The truths she taught me were the same truths the Holy Spirit brought back to my remembrance after I received the Baptism of the Holy Spirit. But what impressed me more than anything else was that she was a servant. I have seen her wash peoples' clothes and do things other people wouldn't do. She wasn't too good to clean, sweep, cook or do whatever needed to be done. Her philosophy, which I hope she instilled in me, and that I have tried to instill in the students in our Bible school, was, "whatsoever your hands find to do, do it." She wore her servant's garment well and blessed many with her poured out life.

THE WOMB OF SERVICE—WORSHIP

Our response to the call to servanthood also depends on our becoming true worshipers of God, for our service is born out of the womb of worship. It is not possible to be rightly motivated or have the attitude of a servant without first being birthed into a relationship of worship to the living God. The Scriptures declare, "Thou shalt worship the Lord thy God, and him only shalt thou serve" (Luke 4:8). That commandment teaches us that worshiping God and serving Him are closely related. We can see the cross in this command. Worshiping the Lord shows our vertical relationship to God, while the horizontal command, "Him only shalt thou serve," stretches us to reach out to mankind. He further taught us that ". . . inasmuch as ye have done it unto one of the least of these my brethren, ye have done it unto me" (Matt. 25:40). Our witness and our worship are determined by our servanthood. *We will worship God no higher than we know Him. We will know Him no higher than we serve Him.* As we worship God our love for Him will grow, and we will desire to find ways to serve Him in order to express that love.

There are fourteen ways given in Scripture to express worship with our physical body. However, learning how to express ourselves in fourteen different ways to God is not necessarily worship. Worship is a way of life, the result of serving. The highest worship

is the given life of a servant. Paul declared, "I beseech
you therefore, brethren, by the mercies of God, that ye
present your bodies a living sacrifice, holy, acceptable
unto God, which is your reasonable service" (Rom.
12:1). He is not speaking of simply coming to church to
give a sacrifice of the fruit of our lips in praising God,
but of our very lives becoming a sacrifice. If our lives
are a living sacrifice, worship will be a spontaneous
overflow of who we are.

Service is an evidence of the way we worship. When
we serve the body of Christ we show that we love God.
There is no way we can love Him and not serve our fel-
low man, as well as our brothers and sisters in the
Church. My Father has shown me that when I stand
before Him, the rewards I receive for every service I
have conducted and every life I have touched will be
shared by Fountain Gate Ministries, Shekinah Ministries and others who have become a part of our service for God. These ministries had a part in sending
me out and they pray for me. We are servants
together. If we serve with singleness of motive, doing
the will of God with our whole soul, we will have as
much reward as those whom we think have done
something greater than we have done. If we serve a
prophet, we share the prophet's reward (Matt. 10:41).
True worship is costly; it costs our lives poured out as
servants to do anything for Jesus, night or day, that
He asks us to do.

GOD IDENTIFIES HIS LEADERS AS SERVANTS

Understanding how God refers to His chosen leaders will help to transform our thinking from the worldly pursuit of greatness. Very often God refers to great men as His servants. Although many great things were written about David, in the New Testament he is called David, the servant of God (Luke 1:69). Moses, the great deliverer of Israel, is spoken of as "My servant Moses" (Josh. 1:1). God was not demeaning the worth of this mighty deliverer, as we might think, but commending him in his relationship to God. To become a servant of God had required great transformation of Moses' character. He had to be changed before he received God's commendation as the meekest man on earth. Joshua, Moses' successor, is called Moses' servant. We may assume that he learned much about leadership from Moses.

The prophet Elisha served Elijah faithfully before receiving his request for a double portion of Elijah's spirit. We read that Elisha poured water on Elijah's hands. What a lowly job, keeping the hands of the prophet clean. But the hour came when the old prophet asked his young servant what he could do for him. Elisha asked for a double portion of Elijah's spirit and received it from God. Servants receive mantles and double portions.

The apostle Paul, in expressing his service to the church at Ephesus, bowed himself in humility and said that with many tears and temptations he *served* his people (Acts 20:19). If it can be said of me when I leave this world, "She was a woman full of the Spirit of the Lord who served God without guile," that would be the greatest compliment anyone could give me. I would rather people did not speak of what I did, but of who I was, a woman with the family spirit, a faithful servant.

Jesus became the Servant in eternity before He came to earth; His very nature is that of a Servant. That which He did in eternity was reflected in the washing of His disciples' feet during His last supper with them. Are we willing to allow the servant attitude expressed by Jesus to be ours? Are we willing to "stoop" to that which is a reversal of the world's system? The world doesn't wash feet. Will we choose to have the family spirit? After Jesus chose to take the seven steps downward, God exalted Him and gave Him a Name that is above every name (Phil. 2:9). Everyone who humbles himself shall be exalted.

I feel I am highly honored to have the privilege of sharing with so many of my Father's family and to meet so many precious brothers and sisters, as well as God's chosen ministers. I never dreamed I would go where I have been able to go or that God would give me the honor to serve where I have had the privilege of serving. I have the honor of bearing my Master's name and I want to be known as His servant. The greatest thing we can aspire to on earth is to be classified by God as *His servant*. Then we'll hear Him say, "Henceforth I call you not servants . . . I call you friends" (John 15:14). The love slave with the bored ear will hear what is in the Father's heart and be a part of fulfilling God's dream, for God talks to His friends.

KNOWING THE MASTER

A servant can best represent his master if he knows him well. When he stays close to the master, a servant understands all his master's moods and knows what he likes and doesn't like. He knows the master better than anyone else.

One precious girl who worked for me is as dear to me as any sister on earth. Gracie worked for me for six years when I pastored in North Carolina. She had another job from three o'clock to eleven o'clock each night. But she became my friend, and said, "My pastor needs me." Every morning by eight o'clock she would arrive at my home. Until one o'clock every day she took care of me and my household, my child and all the guests. At that time I had not yet been healed from an illness that threatened my life, and I spent much of my time in the hospital. Many times Gracie came by the house late at night or in the wee hours of the morning, picked me up, bathed me and held me when I fainted. She had a true servant heart and was a trusted friend.

Years later, when my first husband went to heaven, she came to my home and asked my son, "Is your mommy here?" My son said, "Yes, and she is going to be delighted to see you." He told me that Gracie was there to see me and brought her right in. I said, "Gracie, wasn't my husband a wonderful man?" She looked at me and said, "Nobody knows like you and I know."

Who is going to represent our Master—hirelings or "big shots"? There is a spirit in every one of us that wants to rule. If you don't believe it, get into a car with six people to go eat lunch and see who decides where to go. There is a spirit in man that wants to rule woman, because that is the fallen nature. If we women can't get our way "legitimately," we will try pouting. We all want to be "in charge." Christians should have a totally different spirit from the spirit that wants to rule. The spirit of the family is a servant spirit. If we are going to be like our Father when we get home, we will have to let the Holy Spirit develop in us the spirit of the servant. Another way of describing it is a *lamb spirit.*

The spirit of the household is not one of *independence.* God told me He had kicked the spirit of independence out of heaven, and He won't let it back in. We say the first sin is pride; but it is not. Pride is a result of independence and wanting to rule. All sin comes out of the desire to rule and to be worshiped. No wonder God wants us to become servants. Servanthood will solve the sin question. Having a servant spirit will destroy the sin principle at work in us. We won't have a servant spirit unless we take our self-life to the cross, and there exchange our self-life for the Christ-life. We say we would like to have the Spirit of Christ. Do we mean that? The Spirit of Christ is the spirit of a servant who by choice humbled Himself. Someone said he prayed for God to make him humble. God doesn't do that. He tells us to humble *ourselves*, and He will exalt us (James 4:10). A servant is someone who stoops low enough to be great enough to receive the family spirit.

Our homes will be transformed into refuges of peace and comfort when we lay down our desire to rule and humble ourselves to respond to the call to servant-hood. Then we will begin to know what God planned for the home and family, and to walk in His divine order for mankind that will make our days as days of heaven on earth.

6

The Candidates for God's Dream

God Made Them Adam

That people often study their Bibles through eyes of prejudice, custom and tradition is one of the deep concerns of my heart. They read into the Scriptures what they have been taught, instead of *coming in faith* with an open heart and mind to hear what the Holy Spirit meant. The apostle Paul declared that ". . . before faith came, we were kept under the law, shut up unto the faith which should afterwards be revealed" (Gal. 3:23). People can't understand the Word until they have revealed faith, because tradition, prejudice, culture, denominationalism, pseudo-masculinism and other bondages of the carnal mind hinder them. After that faith comes, we are no longer under the law, but walk in the grace Jesus brought to us through redemption. Paul further told the Galatians, "But after that faith is come, we are no longer under a schoolmaster. For ye are all the children of God by faith in Christ Jesus" (Gal. 3:25-26). Then he added: "There is neither Jew nor Greek, there is neither bond nor free, there is neither male nor female: for ye are all one in Christ Jesus" (Gal. 3:28).

Faith comprehends God's intentions in creating mankind. The fall of man has so damaged us that we are quite unaware of the purpose for which God created man. We are oblivious to the divine order that He intended that man and woman enjoy. Until faith comes to our hearts we cannot expect an illumination of the Word of God that gives us understanding of the purposes of God. The Scriptures teach that "the natural man receiveth not the things of the Spirit of God: for they are foolishness unto him: neither can he know them, because they are spiritually discerned" (I Cor. 2:14). We should not wonder, then, that the Church, which has not yet come into a proper relationship with the Holy Spirit, is living without true understanding of God's divine order for mankind.

A basic misunderstanding arises from our definition of "man." In the Hebrew, the word "man" has no gender to it, but is translated as our word "mankind." "And the Lord God said, It is not good that the man should be alone; I will make him an help meet for him" (Gen. 2:18). Now God is going to do surgery to separate mankind into two sexes. In mankind was "male" and "female." We don't understand male and female if we don't understand "mankind." When God made a help meet for Adam, He caused a deep sleep to fall upon him. Then He took one of Adam's ribs, from that rib made a woman and brought her unto the man. Adam said, "This is now bone of my bones, and flesh of my flesh: she shall be called Woman, because she was taken out of Man" (Gen. 2:23). The next verse teaches that God's purpose was for them to be one. God brought the woman *unto* the man, not *under* him. She was to walk beside him and be one with him. God ordained that woman should be a "help meet" for the man. One of the Hebrew words for "help meet" is "reflection." That is a beautiful picture of God's divine intention in creating mankind to walk together as one in fellowship with God.

The woman was not named Eve until after they fell by disobedience to God's command. God did not name the woman. Adam named her Eve after the fall, so the fallen woman is "Eve." As God's plan for redemption unfolds, we realize that to be a part of the bride of Christ, we must be redeemed from that fallen "Eve" nature. Christ is going to take a wife, but she is not going to be "Eve." We are born again in Christ, Who is called the "last Adam," to become one with Him, redeemed from the curse that came upon mankind because of disobedience.

The serpent beguiled the woman in the garden, and she and her husband partook of the forbidden tree. After that, "they heard the voice of the Lord God walking in the garden in the cool of the day: and Adam and his wife hid themselves from the presence of the Lord God amongst the trees of the garden" (Gen. 3:8). Both the man and the woman heard God coming and hid from Him. It is interesting that in our tradition and prejudice we say the woman cannot hear God, that man must hear Him and tell the woman what He said. The Scriptures do not teach that as God's divine order for mankind. Adam and his wife fellowshipped together with the Voice of God in the garden until the time of their disobedience. We do not know how long they lived before falling to sin, but God visited them until then.

Both genders of mankind were confronted by God and received separate judgments because of their wrongdoing. Adam "pointed the finger" at his wife when God confronted him, declaring, "The woman whom thou gavest to be with me, she gave me of the tree, and I did eat" (Gen. 3:12). Here began the tragic controversy between the sexes that has raged mercilessly throughout the history of man. It has run from the extremes of so demeaning woman in some cultures that she is of less value than animals, to demanding in other cultures that she be given the status of man in every way, thereby threatening the very basis of womanhood. There is little peace or harmony in the best of situations between male and female, much less the "oneness" that God declared as His intention for mankind. Even in the Church, where redemption is working, we still come short of Paul's declaration that in Christ there is neither male nor female. We continue to speak to "issues" regarding the acceptable role of women in the ministry of the Church, demonstrating that we have not "come to faith." We have accepted the plight of fallen man as God's divine order for the Church.

When God confronted the woman because of her disobedience, He indicated several ways she would suffer as a fallen woman. In speaking of the serpent, He said, "And I will put enmity between thee and the woman, and between thy seed and her seed; it shall bruise thy head, and thou shalt bruise his heel" (Gen. 3:15). I believe the devil hates women more than men. God didn't say He would put enmity between the serpent and the man. The enmity is between the serpent and the woman, because the woman's seed would eventually crush the devil. Even in this judgment for sin, however, a loving God is speaking His promise of redemption. He determined to use a virgin to bear the Son that would bruise satan's head. Then the devil hated the woman because she was going to bring forth the Son, and now he hates the Church, because she is going to bring forth the Son again. As we have mentioned, especially where Christianity is not part of a culture, women have suffered terrible abuse through the centuries, under the influence of satanically inspired cultures. Every time a woman gives birth to a baby, God's family has the possibility of being enlarged. (We should not wonder who is influencing the zero birth rate trend of many nations, convincing couples not to have children.)

God continued addressing the fallen woman, saying, "I will greatly multiply thy sorrow and thy conception; in sorrow thou shalt bring forth children; and thy desire shall be to thy husband, and he shall rule over thee" (Gen. 3:16). God was not revealing His divine order for the woman, but imposing on her the consequences of her fall. He was telling us how a *fallen* man and woman were going to relate to each other.

The fallen man would rule the woman, and she would desire him. In today's culture we see the fallen woman chasing the man more blatantly than ever. The natural woman feels she has to have a man, not to be a help meet to him as was purposed in the beginning, but to tempt and allure him through her passion and lust with the goal of controlling him. And the natural man's desire is to conquer the woman, to rule over her. That is all part of fallen life. So the woman must prepare to live under the fallen man, because as long as he is fallen, he will seek to rule over her. It is amazing that even in the Church, we have accepted as divine order for the home the premise that men are to rule their households. That is not in the Book, but is the desire of the fallen nature. Results of the fall of man can never be construed as God's divine order for him. God told Adam he was going to eat by the sweat of his brow, but that was a consequence of sin rather than God's divine intention for him. God had purposed that mankind eat of the vegetation in the beautiful garden He had prepared for them and have dominion over every living thing.

In the garden, man was neither moral nor immoral, but was created amoral. He was given the power of choice, because God wanted us to choose to love Him freely, not out of compulsion. Mankind failed the love test when the first pair disobeyed the command of God not to eat of the tree of the knowledge of good and evil. Through their wrong choice, mankind became immoral. But God's eternal plan was not thwarted, for He had anticipated Adam's failure before the foundation of the world and had prepared a Savior for mankind.

John assures us: "For this purpose was the Son of God manifested, that he might destroy the works of the devil" (I John 3:8). That word "destroy" is the Greek word *louso*, which means "to loose, to undo, outdo and overdo"; so are we to destroy everything the devil has ever done. When we accept Christ as our

Savior, we are restored to the image of God. Restoration is a wonderful reality which promises that we will become all that God ordained for us to become in His eternal purpose.

My son, Darrell, has a hobby of restoring old cars. When they are completely restored, they are perfect representations of what the designers intended them to be, no matter how decrepit they were when the work of restoration began. If we can believe that God is perfectly restoring us to His image to reflect His will, we can rejoice even in our trials. We will experience what mankind would have known if the first pair had walked on with God and not fallen.

There was nothing to which Jesus laid the ax more violently than the traditions of men. Because of bondage to tradition, some cannot understand that there is no difference between male and female, for they have not come to faith. Paul declared that when we come to faith we will understand that there is neither Greek or Barbarian, nor male or female, but we are all one in Christ Jesus. God is preparing men and women alike to be filled with His Spirit in the fullness of time, and is delivering us from tradition, prejudice, culture and denominationalism.

We have tried to lay a guilt trip on men by telling them they are to fulfill every desire and deepest need of a woman. Men have been put into bondage by the expectation of their wives to meet every need of their lives. Though husbands should meet the physical and emotional needs of their wives, they cannot be expected to meet their spiritual needs. That is not God's divine order. Both man and woman are to walk together as one and let God fulfill the cry of their spirits for a true Bridegroom.

Many men have been gloriously delivered from the burden that some marriage counselors put upon them to meet their wife's every need. That was not God's intention. God ordained that man and woman should walk with Him and be as one, and He would meet the innermost needs of both of them. Divine order is higher than the plight of fallen man. It is far more liberating to men and women than having to live under the doctrine of the curse of a fallen Adam and a fallen Eve.

We have been redeemed to be one flesh in Him, bought with a price so that husbands and wives can truly become one. Paul admonished us:

> . . . *submitting yourselves one to another in the fear of God. Wives, submit yourselves unto your own husbands, as unto the Lord. For the husband is the head of the wife, even as Christ is the head of the church: and he is the saviour of the body. Therefore as the church is subject unto Christ, so let the wives be to their own husbands in every thing* (Eph. 5:21-24).

God said the husband is the head of the wife. We have called him the priest of the home, but the Bible

does not teach that. The Bible teaches we are all part
of a royal priesthood, to "shew forth the praises of him
who hath called you out of darkness into his marvel-
lous light" (I Pet. 2:9). To say the husband is the "head"
and not the "priest" is not a matter of semantics; it is
a matter of assignment, of delegated authority. And I
tell the men they don't want me to preach about their
delegated authority, because being the head of the
home involves much more than being a priest. That
wonderful realm of authority that God delegated is
marvelous. But we must not give the man authority
God didn't give him, or take away the authority that
God did give him. God did not mean to put one gender
of mankind over another, but for them to walk
together as one, submitting themselves one to another.

This understanding does not destroy the order of
the home; it does not touch delegated authority; it does
not make women higher than men, or make them
agressive or domineering. It puts man and woman
back together in Jesus. We do not need "Women's Lib"
or ERA. They are only swapping places to rule instead
of fallen man, who was not supposed to be ruling
anyway. I want to be redeemed to God's purpose for
mankind to become who I was made to be in God and
walk beside the man with whom I am supposed to
walk. In Christ, now, there is neither male nor female,
but mankind, walking together.

After the fall of man, when Adam named his wife
Eve, we read, "This is the book of the generations of

Adam . . . and Adam lived an hundred and thirty years, and begat a son in his own likeness, *after his image* . . ." (Gen. 5:1,3) Here we see the generation of Adam, not Jesus. And he begat sons in his own image. We were born in the nature of Adam. The carnal nature comes from our father Adam, not from our Father God. God knew we couldn't change ourselves back into His image, so He designed the costly plan of redemption through the blood of His own Son, Jesus. I spent seventeen years trying to act like Him. Two thirds of the Church world today is trying to "act" like Jesus. We don't have that ability. Jesus was the express image of the Father, sent to live in us by the power of the Holy Spirit until that image takes over our inner natures—our spirits and souls. He begins to change us from glory to glory. When He fills our beings, as He wanted to do before man ever fell, we are going to go home in His image, complete and mature.

The more I am willing to give up my image, the more of God's image I can receive. "Good-bye, Adam. Today I'm not going to have your image. I do not vote for you; you are dead and dead people don't talk. Today the image of God is going to be allowed to operate in my life." Being changed from glory to glory is not the same as being challenged. Being challenged won't take you home in His image; only change will do that. By the action of Calvary, we are being changed into Christ's image so male and female can walk together as one, each with his or her own delegated authority.

God puts both of them back into Christ; not as male and female, but as mankind, walking with God. Husband and wife, male and female preacher, man and woman leader will walk in the cool of the day with Jesus Who is talking to us, fellowshipping with us, giving us authority and changing us into His image. In the last Adam, God is restoring what we would have had if Adam had not fallen in the beginning. It is glorious indeed to see God restoring men and women together "as one," seeing them fulfill their delegated responsibilities, yet both being the servants that He has called them to be.

As God delivers His Church from the bondages of tradition and culture and from fallen man's doctrine of divine order, we will see men and women function together to build godly homes and to fulfill God's purpose for the building of His Church. As redemption cleanses us from the desire to rule, man and woman will not be threatened by each other, but will welcome the godly counsel of one another.

The Bible gives many examples of women who provided godly leadership. Deborah was set by God as a judge, a prophetess and a general in the army. She was able to tell Barak what God had said to her, and Barak then declared he would not go to battle without her (Judg. 4:4-8). Deborah was a woman who knew where to be and when to be, and who stayed with God until the right time came. I believe in these last days of God's outpouring of His Spirit, many Baraks will say to their Deborahs that they will not go to battle without them. I feel it is the timing of God to restore man and woman back to the divine order in the home and in the Kingdom of God. I believe they will walk together as one under God's mandate, to tend the garden, multiply, take dominion over every living thing, and, as the bride of Christ, prepare for His coming. It is the hour for man and woman to come to faith, to stop living under fallen doctrine, and to start living according to divine order.

In the last five years I have begun to see some interesting changes in the Church. More men and women are working together as co-pastors than I have seen in all my previous years of ministry. Men who are being restored are realizing there are two of us, and no one is usurping the other's delegated authority. God pours out His Spirit on His sons and His daughters alike. We are in Christ, the last Adam Who didn't fail, and in Him everything is being restored to fulfill God's dream.

7

The Crucible of God's Dream

Cleansing His Church

The truths that Jesus taught through parables are like stones thrown into a mirrored pond, creating ever-widening ripples on the water. The physical elements of the parables are like the stones, and the truths they teach like the ripples on the water. The Holy Spirit has come to lead us into all truth. As we cultivate our relationship with Him, He opens the Scriptures to give greater understanding than we have previously grasped.

Sometimes we have seen only the "stones" of truth and not comprehended the larger meaning reflected in the "ripples." For example, in the parable of the lost sheep, the lost coin, and the lost son (Luke 15), many of his hearers saw only the physical elements of the story. They understood that a shepherd was concerned enough for his lost sheep that he left the others to go and find it, and they rejoiced with the woman who lost her coin and swept until she found it. They empathized with a father's heart whose son had left and was now returning, but did not see beyond the literal characters of the story to the truth Jesus was teaching.

Others have seen the first few ripples on the water and applied their understanding to the significance of the lost sheep representing a lost sinner for whom the Chief shepherd searches until He brings him safely home. Likewise, with the lost coin, and the lost son, we have applied this truth to lost sinners finding their way home to God. That is certainly a valid understanding, for Jesus came to "seek and to save that which was lost." However, the Holy Spirit is enlarging our understanding of truth and giving us prophetic insight into what Jesus was teaching that applies specifically to the Church today.

The stories of the lost sheep, the lost coin and the lost son actually comprise one parable. When Jesus' presence drew a crowd, the Scripture says He spoke *this* parable to them. Although the parable includes three different subjects, we must relate them to a single truth that Jesus was teaching in order to fully understand His intent. The complete significance of what Jesus was teaching will be captured only as we grasp the composite picture He painted in the entire parable. As the Holy Spirit opens our understanding, we lose sight of the physical elements of these picture stories and begin to see clearly a larger truth regarding the fulfillment of God's dream for His Church. Jesus never lost sight of the ultimate purpose for which He had come, and every word He spoke related to the fulfilling of that purpose.

In this parable, Jesus gave a beautiful prophetic word concerning what will happen in the Church Age. He began by describing a shepherd who has lost a sheep:

> *What man of you, having an hundred sheep, if he lose one of them, doth not leave the ninety and nine in the wilderness, and go after that which is lost, until he find it? And when he hath found it, he layeth it on his shoulders, rejoicing. And when he cometh home, he calleth together his friends and neighbours, saying unto them, Rejoice with me; for I have found my sheep which was lost. I say unto you, that likewise joy shall be in heaven over one sinner that repenteth, more than over ninety and nine just persons, which need no repentance* (Luke 15:4-7).

Jesus refers to Himself as the good Shepherd who lays down His life for His sheep. The Scriptures often refer to Christ's followers as sheep. Peter exhorts elders of the church to feed the "flock" of God, promising that ". . . when the chief Shepherd shall appear, ye shall receive a crown of glory that fadeth not away" (I Pet. 5:2,4). So we may consider the Church to be a sheepfold where there is safety and care for each sheep, as well as food and provision. Sheep require much care because they are among the dumbest animals in the world, capable of wandering away, losing their direction and getting themselves into dangerous situations. They need the care of a shepherd. Jesus is the chief Shepherd, and He has given pastors to the Church who have shepherds' hearts. They will care for His sheep, feed them and protect them from wolves and other enemies.

God is bringing the Church back to the leadership of the Chief Shepherd, under whom He places an under-shepherd. I am referring to a true shepherd who leads a local church, rather than a dominating ruler who dictates his will to people. There is a vast difference between dictatorship and true leadership. A true shepherd leads, feeds, protects and cares for the sheep. God places true shepherds where He wants them for as long as He needs them, and moves them when His purposes are accomplished. He declares them to be a gift to the Church (Eph. 4:10). Revival is coming to the Church, not to "free lancers" who say they don't need a church. God is intent on putting sheep under a shepherd because every sheep needs a sheepfold. The hour has come when we must be established in the local church, listen to the voice of the Chief Shepherd, and be led by under-shepherds.

The shepherd in this parable put the lost sheep on his shoulders and carried her home. The original language gave the beautiful understanding that when the shepherd put the lost sheep on his shoulders, he carried her home safe and sound, fully restored. The shoulder, as generally used in Scripture, represents strength, succor, security, soundness, serenity and the sovereignty of government. The prophet Isaiah wrote of Jesus, "But he was wounded for our transgressions, he was bruised for our iniquities: the chastisement of our peace was upon him; and with his stripes we are healed. All we like sheep have gone astray . . . and the Lord hath laid on him the iniquity of us all" (Isa. 53:5-6). Jesus' back bore the pain of a cruel beating so that we could know healing.

I believe with all my heart that the days ahead are going to be days of great healing, for Jesus is not only going to heal peoples' bodies, but their psyches and their homes. I am weary of people nursing and justifying their hurts. It doesn't matter if they inherited it from grandma or grandpa, or how long they have had it; whether it was child abuse, or a wound inflicted by the church or preacher. I believe if we appropriate the provision of the wounded shoulder of the Shepherd, we can go home healed, safe and sound. It will be beautiful to see the Shepherd pick up His wandering sheep, the Church, put her on His shoulder and arrive home, restored to all He has purposed for her.

Jesus continued His teaching:

> *Either what woman, having ten pieces of silver, if she lose one piece, doth not light a candle, and sweep the house, and seek diligently till she find it? And when she hath found it, she calleth her friends and her neighbours together, saying, Rejoice with me; for I have found the piece which I had lost. Likewise, I say unto you, there is joy in the presence of the angels of God over one sinner that repenteth* (Luke 15:8-10).

The parable now introduces a good woman who has lost one of her ten pieces of silver. In order to grasp the significance of her loss, we must understand what that silver coin represented. In Jesus' day married women did not wear wedding rings as we do today to represent a covenant vow of faithfulness between a man and woman who marry. According to Bible custom, a virtuous married woman wore a necklace containing ten pieces of silver. That necklace was significant because it identified her as a virtuous woman.

If a woman was caught in adultery, she was brought to the gates of the city, and there the rulers of the city took off one piece of her silver. When people saw her on the street without the tenth piece of silver in her necklace, they recognized her as an adulteress. If through carelessness she lost a piece of her silver, her reputation as a virtuous woman was threatened. That is why the woman called for a light and a broom and swept until she found her lost coin. She wasn't about to go outside her home with nine pieces of silver around her neck and have everyone who saw her label her an adulteress.

Bible scholars generally agree that the "good woman" in the Scriptures represents the Church in type. The woman in this parable was a good woman who through carelessness had lost her identity. The Church at one time wore her label of holiness and chastity and lived a life that was different from the way the rest of the world lived. In the days of Charles Finney, people tipped their hats as he walked down the street because of the solemnity of the anointing that was upon this man of God. When he walked into a factory, people fell to the ground because of the power of the Holy Spirit that was on his life. Taverns shut down, movies went out of business, and godliness prevailed over worldliness in whole cities. A study of revivals throughout history reveals similar results in many lives and even entire cities being transformed to godly lifestyles.

Today the Church is being shamed in the media and before the world because of the reproach that has been brought by religious leaders who have lost their identification of holiness and righteousness. Many in the Church have decided they want to look, smell and walk like people in the world who don't know God. Through carelessness, apathy and compromise with the world, the Church has lost her piece of silver, and is bearing the reproach of being adulterous. We need to do as the woman in the parable and call for a light and a broom and begin to sweep until we regain possession of our lost silver, our identification as a holy people.

Scripture refers to silver as a type of redemption. Malachi writes, "And he shall sit as a refiner and purifier of silver: and he shall purify the sons of Levi, and purge them as gold and silver, that they may offer unto the Lord an offering in righteousness" (Mal. 3:3). God is putting His Church into a crucible of circumstances and applying heat to allow the dross to come to the top and be purged. Jesus is coming for a holy Church, not a worldly one. The message of holiness is sounding loud and clear in the Church, for God is calling His people to repent of carelessness and compromise with the world to walk in faithfulness with Jesus, their true Bridegroom.

The woman in the parable diligently swept the house until she found her silver that was lost. We see the Church being swept as God is tearing down men's kingdoms and exposing sin. It is incredible what the light of the Holy Spirit exposes. Revival starts with housecleaning, shaking and cleansing. We must quit being religious so we can truthfully say, "It is not the preacher or the deacon, but it's me, O Lord, standing in the need of prayer. I need a broom and a light. Inside me there are things that I have been covering up, places where I have compromised, so that I have lost my identification as a faithful follower of Christ. The world doesn't recognize me as different from them."

Identification is one of the greatest doctrines of the Bible; it matters that we are who we say we are. It doesn't matter what people think of us or how religious we are. *What matters is who we are in the presence of God.* The beginning of revival is calling for a light, then sweeping, cleaning, repenting. May we be willing to ask God to send the light into our spirits for Him to show us what is there. Then when that white light of God's judgment comes inside of us, we are going to know where to sweep with the broom. We must spend time being honest before God. If there is dirt in our temple, something we don't want the Lord to see, let's call for the broom. Many people have a lot of dirt they are excusing by blaming their husband or wife or saying they have been this way all their lives. "My mother was this way; my daddy was this way." We don't belong to that daddy any longer. We belong to the family of God. We know we need to be cleansed and washed to have revival and be restored to our true identification.

Jesus concluded this parable by telling of the lost son.

> *A certain man had two sons: And the younger
> of them said to his father, Father, give me the
> portion of goods that falleth to me. And so he
> divided unto them his living. And not many days
> after the younger son gathered all together and
> took a journey into a far country, and there
> wasted his substance with riotous living* (Luke
> 15:11-13).

This boy was a *son* living in the Father's house. We
have heard it taught that he was a sinner who came
home to God. The message can be applied in that way,
giving us a revelation of the loving Father's heart that
is ready to forgive. However, as we consider the fact
that this boy was a son, leaving home with the gifts he
received from the Father, we can see more clearly
what has happened in the Church.

As a son he did something foolish. He asked his
father to give him the inheritance he was entitled to
receive, which the father did. It was the younger son
who decided to leave, the one who was less mature. In
his immaturity, he perhaps thought he had all he
needed in the gifts the father gave him, and that he
could live better without the father's interference. The
father's heart must have ached, but because of his
desire to have a son who was mature, he let him go.

There was an attitude in many who were involved
in the Charismatic Move of God that closely parallels
the attitude of this younger son. The gifts of God were

supremely important, as well as ministries and inheritances. People felt it was within their rights as sons of God to demand material prosperity as well as spiritual gifts and to develop their own ministries. The Bible says the younger son went out and spent his inheritance in riotous living. That is, he was hilariously living it up. Many pastors have had people come to us who said they felt led to go out and exercise *their own ministry*. They took their portion, their inheritance or gifts, and put up signs all over the city: "Man of Power: Come and see my Miracles." The more spectacular their miracles were, the more people followed them.

I am not discounting the work of the Holy Spirit in the Charismatic Move, for thousands of lives were brought into a new experience of reality during that time. However, the attitude I am describing prevailed among many who were involved in Charismatic ministries. It is true that we all have a right to the inheritance and we have received gifts. The Holy Spirit brought twenty-one gifts to the Church when He came, and they belong to us. But too often we have become enthralled with the gifts and have lost sight of the Giver. How much better it would have been for the younger son to have stayed at home with the father. Instead, he squandered his wealth, and when famine came he had nothing to eat. The Charismatic Move has come to an end, and many find themselves empty and hungry, with nothing to eat.

Many in the Church have gone down to the swine pen to feed on husks. When someone preaches on the radio that if you will send him twenty dollars he will send you a string to tie around your waist so you can lose weight, that is a pigpen. When they offer to sell water from the Jordan where John baptized as holy water, or offer to send oil from a tree that was used to anoint Elijah, that is a disgrace. That is not preaching the living Word, which is bread for the hungry soul. The Book tells us the son "came to his senses." Some will have to go by way of the pigpen to come to their senses. Some who do go that way will be too proud to repent. However, there are those who are humbling themselves, repenting and being restored.

Now the Church is getting hungry for the Word, for fresh bread that comes from the Father's house. "When he came to his senses," this son realized that the servants in his father's house had bread to eat while he was starving in a pigpen. Coming to his senses brought him to an attitude of repentance. This is the hour that repentance must come to the Church. More than just saying, "I am sorry," repentance is letting God break our hearts over our sins until we are willing to confess, "Father, I have sinned against God and the Church; I have been more interested in myself and my ministry than anything else. I am hungry, and no one can satisfy me except You, because there is a place created in me for God that no one else can fill." Hallelujah! The Church is coming home to the Father.

This time we will not be satisfied with knowing the redemptive work of our Lord or the gifts of the Holy Spirit. I believe the next revelation coming to the Church will be a revelation of our Father. Jesus came to unveil the Father to us.

When the boy came to his senses he was willing to return to his father's house as a *servant*, saying he was no longer worthy to be called a son. His tone was totally different now; the strut had been taken out of him. He was not flipping his Bible, saying, "Look at me, I'm the person God raised up and no one else in the world can do what I can do." He had been stripped and was returning with his head down, crying, "I'm hungry, and I am going back to my daddy's house." He wanted to sit down with his father and eat with him. When we are willing to be made servants, the Father's house will open to us. The father had to let this boy go to the swine pen and exhaust all his gifts, his power and anointing, before he finally came to himself. When he had exhausted his resources and was starving to death in the swine pen, he thought of father's house and could almost smell the fresh bread being prepared there. He arose to make the journey home, defeated, broken and humiliated, ready to become a servant in His father's house. However, he could not have anticipated the reception that awaited him there.

"But when he was yet a great way off, the father saw him and had compassion" (v 20). The father had been watching for his son, aching in his own heart because of the suffering he knew his son must be experiencing. Not only was the father watching for him, he had gifts to give to him as well. These gifts were far better than those the son required when he left home, because they would last forever. When he saw his son trudging his weary way home, the father ran to him and *kissed* him. The gift of that kiss of reconciliation meant that everything was all right between them.

The kiss is one of the most beautiful ways to express deep, intimate love. There is nothing on earth as wonderful as knowing that there has been a reconciliation between you and your father. One of my greatest experiences in God was the first time I was able to say to my heavenly Father, "Please put Your arms around me and let me feel Your kiss." After being born again, loving God with all my heart and preaching the old-fashioned Methodist faith for nineteen years, I trembled the first time I ever asked Him to do that for fear it was blasphemous. But something inside me cried out for my heavenly "Daddy" to put His arms around me.

We had been having a move of God for about a week in our Bible school, with the students and faculty praying around the clock. I had been waiting in the presence of God and I cried out to Him, "Please put Your arms around me." I felt His kiss; then I understood the cry of the bride in the Song of Solomon, "Kiss me with your kisses" (Song of Sol. 1:2). When He kissed me, He left with me His Word. The day is coming when the Church is going to receive the kiss of reconciliation from the Father and know deeper revelation of His Word.

Then the Father requested that the *best robe* be brought to His repentant son. This robe was special, one the Father had been saving. In many countries, when a king gets ready to take a bride, he has a special dress made for her with a beautiful design embroidered around the bottom and around the sleeves and neck that matches the design of his own robe. It has the crest, the government seal, everything that is on his robe, but is made in a smaller design to fit her. When she stands beside him to be presented as the queen, she has on a robe designed exactly like the king's robe. Our Father has been working on a bride's dress, and the bride has been working on it too. "She shall be brought to the king in raiment of fine needlework" (Ps. 45:14). She has been embroidering it with the threads of the trials of her life, and every thread she has woven in her testings has embroidered His image into her robe. One day when the Bridegroom presents His bride, she will be found wearing His robe.

Then the father said, "Bring the *ring.*" In Scripture, the ring signifies authority as a power of attorney. Joseph was given the ring of Pharaoh, and with it the power of second-in-command. In the Book of Esther, the king's ring was taken from wicked Haman and given to Mordecai, who is a type of the Holy Spirit, ruling in righteousness. The ring was dipped into hot wax and pressed onto a written decree. According to the law, any decree sealed with the stamp of the king's ring could not be reversed.

Our Father is going to put a ring on the Church's finger. He is calling us to prayer, getting ready for the Holy Spirit to stamp with hot wax His answer to the "fervent prayer of the righteous man that availeth much" (James 5:16). That is "hot wax" prayer. He is going to let the Church take the ring that He puts on her finger and use it to answer her prayers. That ring will give us authority over the devil. I believe the Church is going to have power such as we have never known to work miracles. People are going to be healed and delivered as the Church uses her ring of authority to declare that she is taking territory from the devil.

Sandals were a significant gift of the father to his son, for they represented his status of sonship. In Bible times, when someone was disowned and lost his sonship, he took off his shoes. Servants who were not sons did not wear shoes. The Church is called to walk in the light, in love, in the truth, in holiness and in the Spirit. The key word in the Book of Ephesians is the "walk" of the Church, which reveals our sonship.

These gifts were all a vital part of the precious reception the loving Father gave to this prodigal son.

However, receiving the kiss, wearing the robe of righteousness, putting the ring on his finger and having shoes on his feet could not satisfy his *hunger*. The father called for a feast to be made and they rejoiced together around a banquet table over the return of this lost son. The Church is getting ready to have a revival that will feed hungry sons who are returning to the Father's house. They will receive gifts because of their brokenness and willingness to live as servants in the Father's house. With a servant spirit they can enjoy the robe of righteousness and be trusted with the ring of authority. Living in reconciliation with the Father, they will walk in the stature of true sonship.

This younger son had learned, through failure, to value the father's presence and enjoy relationship with him. Unfortunately, the elder son in the parable had not developed that relationship, though he had stayed in the father's house. He became angry and critical of his father's relationship to this younger son who had obviously "blown it." The attitude of the elder brother serves as a warning to many in the Church who are in danger of missing the next move of God. They refuse to go into the banquet to rejoice with the father, even though he comes to request their presence. It seems that every generation in Church history that has experienced a great move of God has failed to go into the next move that God brings. In every move of God some have said, "We don't want to go on. This is not the way we did it fifty years ago."

The director of one of our national Bible colleges was in one of my meetings in New Jersey. After I preached, he stood up and said to me, "I don't know your age, but I would call you a senior saint." He said that he had never seen a senior saint out on the cutting edge of what God is currently doing as he had seen me that day and that most of the older people he knew lived in what "used to be." He continued, "Here is a woman on the edge of prophetic truth who is telling us what is going to happen." He raved on until I was embarrassed, while he stood and declared to everyone present, "I shall not be left behind. I'm going to be on the cutting edge of what God is doing and learn to hear what the Spirit is saying to the Church at this hour." Age doesn't have anything to do with going on with God. What matters is that we are able to see and hear what God is saying and doing. Then we must respond with the joy of the Father's heart in restoring sons to His house, instead of allowing the attitude of the elder brother to rule us.

There was great rejoicing over finding the lost sheep, the lost coin and the lost son. Each time there is a "found" people, there is great rejoicing. The Word teaches us concerning celebration, worship and dancing before the Lord. In the Father's house, there is a banquet with music and merriment to celebrate the joy of His heart at the return of His son. I didn't receive the understanding of celebration in a classroom situation. As I wrote earlier, God healed me from a death bed. I was in braces, and God put my backbone together in seven places. He healed me in a Pentecostal meeting when I was a Methodist preacher, and when God struck me with Holy Ghost power, I danced before the Lord, though I didn't believe in it.

There is a controversy in the Church today about praise and worship. A young pastor made an appointment to see me regarding a difficulty he was having with his leaders. He related to me that he had been reproved by his denominational conference because they did not approve of the praise and worship his church was experiencing. This young pastor showed these men what the Scriptures teach regarding dancing before the Lord and they replied, "We can't help what the Book says, our conference doesn't believe in it." My response to this young minister was, "If the Book says it, I will die by it." We must give up our opinions and notions to accept what the Book says or we will not be a part of the next move of God.

Celebration is part of the revival that is coming, when holiness is restored and sons come home to the Father's house. We must be careful not to demonstrate the attitude of the elder brother and miss what the Father is doing in this hour. Celebration is God's desire for His redeemed Church. The Kingdom of God is "... righteousness, peace, and joy in the Holy Ghost" (Rom. 14:17). The shepherd celebrated the return of the lost sheep, and the woman called her friends to celebrate the finding of her silver. The father said it was right to celebrate because his son was alive again. The more we receive of the family spirit of God, the more we will celebrate our redemption.

The Church is the purpose of God unfolded to fulfill His dream for a family that bears His image. The sacrifice of Calvary has guaranteed that God's dream will be fulfilled, for "... he shall see of the travail of His soul and be satisfied" (Isa. 53:11). Whatever crucible God has to use to cleanse His Church will result, not in destruction, but in redemption to make her a glorious Church without spot or wrinkle. There will be a people who will possess their inheritance and become a part of the culmination of God's dream.

8

The Culmination of God's Dream

The New Generation

The revelation of God's eternal plan opened to another dimension for me recently. God revealed a truth that literally changed my life as He unfolded the mandate I felt to train leaders during this time of transition in the Church. A few months earlier I had left Fountain Gate Ministries, the church I founded and had pastored for seventeen years, to travel extensively in this training ministry. The Bible College of Fountain Gate Ministries was planning their graduation ceremonies the spring following my leaving and invited me to return as pastor emerita to speak to the graduating class. I was delighted to accept the invitation. I had

poured my life into these students and had felt this
particular class had more potential to succeed in God
than any we had previously graduated. I sought God
earnestly to give me a life-changing message for these
students to take with them into their fields of ministry.

Arriving a few days early, my husband and I enjoyed participating in many of the activities before the
graduation ceremony on Sunday night. We were staying in the home of one of the elders of the church, a
precious friend. After we had spent an evening enjoying a meal together, I asked permission to stay in our
hosts' spacious dining room to spend some time seeking God for what He wanted to say to that graduating
class. Of course they granted that permission, and I
spent the late hours of the night waiting on God.

My conversation with my Father began something
like this: "Father, I want You to tell me what You want
me to say to this graduating class. I didn't come here
at the expense of this church just to fill up time and
space." (I have never met anyone who ever remem-
bered his graduation exercise address.) I didn't want
to merely challenge that class, but I wanted them to
leave that school knowing God had spoken to them
and that the message had changed their lives.

As I waited, my Father asked me to talk to Him
about the wilderness through which Moses led the
children of Israel. He wanted me to describe the people

I saw in the wilderness. So I tried to recall everything I had ever learned about the people in the wilderness and proceeded to describe them. They were people who marched out of Egypt under the leadership and sovereignty of the almighty, omnipotent, omniscient, omnipresent God. Before going very far, however, they desired to go back to Egypt. They were murmurers, complainers and faultfinders who rebelled against the eleven sovereign ways that God visited His people to meet their needs. They built the golden calf, refused to believe the voice of the prophets, and died in that wilderness.

After I finished my dismal description of those wilderness people, my Father said He wanted to talk to me about the wilderness in which I was living. He spoke to me concerning the economic status of our country, the political structure and corruption in our government and the religious world that is full of apathy and love for materialism. He spoke of the moral status of this wilderness with its promiscuous sex, the curse of AIDS and the sin of abortion. He gave me a panoramic view of things that are happening in the wilderness of our nation. Then He said, "On two occasions in history I have invaded this world with a deliverer. The first time I invaded the world in answer to My peoples' cry and sent Moses to deliver them from Egypt. When Moses was born, the Egyptians were killing the male babies. The second time I invaded this world, I sent My Son to deliver My people out of darkness. At the time of Jesus' birth there was also a decree to kill the male babies. Both times satan thought he had killed My deliverers. My daughter, I am about to invade the world again, and they are killing babies again. But they are not going to destroy My Deliverer, for He is the Head of the Church, and My plan cannot be thwarted."

When My Father had thoroughly established in my thinking the wilderness in which I was living, He focused my attention again on that historical wilderness, asking me if all I saw in that wilderness were the murmurers, complainers and faultfinders. Then He began to describe another generation that was in that wilderness, one that had been born to the murmurers and complainers, trained by the wilderness testings to depend on God. They knew what it meant to have fresh bread every morning from the Father's hand, and they drank water from the rock. They didn't bow to idols and they were clothed and fed by God, depending on Him for all their needs. My Father instructed me to think about the "Joshua generation" that had conquered the giants of the promised land. "That Joshua generation is alive in your wilderness today," He said, "and they will receive their inheritance and have a part in fulfilling My eternal plan."

I listened intently to what He was saying. It was as though I had never seen that new generation before. The Father declared to me that He was getting ready to take this Joshua generation into the land. We are living in the most exciting time this world has ever known. Our generation has seen the faithfulness and power of the omnipotent, triune God in the middle of this present wilderness, sustaining such a vast number by supplying them daily bread and giving them to drink from the Rock. I can tell young people that they are living in the greatest hour that has ever been known in Church history. They are going to help take this new generation in to possess the inheritance.

Earnestly wanting to understand what He was showing me, I asked my Father, "What *is* the inheritance?" I told Him that I had heard some people refer to the land of Canaan as a "building program" for their church. They call the new facilities their "Canaan." Others refer to the inheritance of the promised land as the victorious, Spirit-filled life. It is true that as individuals we must live holy lives, conquering the "ites" of our self-lives, possessing the land through our obedience. However, that is not the full meaning of receiving our inheritance. Many of our songs and hymns depict Canaan as heaven, the final destination for weary pilgrims. But Canaan land cannot represent heaven, for there are neither giants to conquer in heaven nor battles to win in the presence of the throne of God. I felt I needed a clearer understanding of the reality of the inheritance God had promised to give the Joshua generation of today.

In answer to my question, my Father asked me to go back with Him into the eons of eternity, before time began, and witness the covenant made in the Godhead that was designed to bring to pass their desire for a family. That covenant is the mystery revealed to Paul and is to be fulfilled by the Church, the body of Christ. Paul declared ". . . Christ also loved the church, and gave himself for it; that he might sanctify and cleanse it with the washing of water by the word, that he might present it to himself a glorious church, not having spot, or wrinkle, or any such thing; but that it should be holy and without blemish" (Eph. 5:25-27). Paul taught that Christ is the Head of the Church (Eph. 5:23). He also taught that God gave the five-fold ministry to the Church for the perfecting of the saints, for the edifying of the body of Christ, "Till we all come in the unity of the faith, and of the knowledge of the Son of God, unto a perfect man, unto the measure of the stature of the fulness of Christ" (Eph. 4:13). As un-fathomable as it may seem, the Father is going to have such a family in the Church who will bear His image.

The inheritance that was partially received in Joshua's generation serves as a type of the promise that is going to be fulfilled in reality in this new generation. The time came when God took Moses home and told Joshua He wanted him to take the generation into Canaan that He had been training in the wilderness. The Scripture presents Joshua as a humble man who had no personal goals other than to please God. He dealt with sin immediately and with finality, and for every successful battle he gave God the glory. He was resourceful in courage, strong in faith and wholeheartedly committed to God and His law. As a leader he showed the way without fear, conquering the land and dividing the inheritance. God is still calling men and women today whose hearts are like Joshua's.

There were some arduous tasks assigned to Joshua, some that many of us would not have wanted. It was time for the children of Israel to begin to receive their inheritance if they were willing. They were being confronted with the decision: Were they willing to go into the promised land? According to the Book, we find that the first generation as a whole decided they didn't want to go into the land God had promised them. As a result, they wandered for thirty-nine years and died in the wilderness. They were those who had come out of Egypt but were overcome by the "system" of the wilderness. They do not represent sinners, for they had come out of Egypt to follow God. But they refused to go on into the promised land, and they died in that wilderness.

There are some in the Church today who are being overcome by the system of the world, worshiping golden calves, rebelling and taking part in gossip, criticism, church splits, murmuring and faultfinding. They do not really know their God. They know *about* Him, but they have no intimate relationship with Him. Though they will not return to Egypt, they will surely perish in the wilderness. There are others like Michal, King David's wife, who mocked David when he worshiped hilariously. She was struck with barrenness, the worst curse that could come to a Jewish woman. There are those like the elder son in the backyard of the prodigal's home, who was a murmurer and complainer and did not join the celebration. He was at the father's house, but he did not rejoice with the father at the return of his prodigal son.

No one can keep us from having what God has ordained we can have except ourselves. We are responsible to choose to receive our inheritance. I have never met a man or woman, church or family, nor have I seen a job or profession that is worth my missing God's inheritance. When I understood God's dream, I determined that no one was worth what it would cost me to miss it. When that kind of determination motivates us, we will enter into our inheritance.

The first generation had died without receiving their inheritance, and now God was preparing to take their sons and daughters into the promised land. "And Joshua said, Hereby ye shall know that the living God is among you, and that he will without fail drive out from before you the Canaanites, and the Hittites, and the Hivites, and the Perizzites, and the Girgashites, and the Amorites, and the Jebusites" (Josh. 3:10). The Father's plan was to give them their inheritance by driving out the enemies that dwelt in the land.

God also said, "Every place that the sole of your foot shall tread upon, that have I given unto you" (Josh. 1:3). The command God gave was two-fold. God was going to run out some of the "ites," but Israel had to *possess* the land in order to receive their inheritance. Joshua's generation did not enter into their full inheritance because they didn't conquer all the "ites." Canaan was a type of the real inheritance God ordained for the Church, as the Old Testament is a shadow of that which is to be fulfilled in reality in the New Testament.

When the Holy Spirit told Paul to leave Jerusalem and go to the desert of Arabia, this newly converted apostle was preaching the gospel as he understood it. He had been transformed by the power of God, apprehended to preach to the Gentiles, and he was preaching his Pentecostal message. (Some of our churches are still doing that.) God had apprehended Paul for more than that, however, for He had been waiting since before the foundation of the world to reveal His mystery to the heart of man.

In that desert, Paul had an encounter with the infinite, almighty, omnipotent God who rolled out His eternal plan and revealed it to this apostle "born out of due season." The Old Testament Book of Joshua has its fulfillment in Paul's letter to the Ephesians in the New Testament. The heart of God was unveiled to Paul concerning the mystery that had been hidden in

God since before the foundation of the world. God had cherished in His heart from eternity His desire for a family, and He revealed to Paul that desire and His plan to fulfill it through the Church. That which God ordained is contained in the Biblical words "predestination," "fore-ordination," "pre-determination," "precounsel" and "elect," as well as other similar words. Paul said he was apprehended that he might preach that mystery that was with God from the beginning and not able to be revealed until now.

The Church is going to receive its inheritance ". . . according to the eternal purpose which He purposed in Christ Jesus" (Eph. 3:11). Paul declared:

> *I became a servant of this gospel by the gift of God's grace given me through the working of His power . . . to preach to the Gentiles the unsearchable riches of Christ, and to make plain to everyone the administration of this mystery, which for ages past was kept hidden in God . . . His intent was that now, through the* **church,** *the manifold wisdom of God should be made known to the rulers and authorities in the heavenly realms, according to his eternal purpose which He accomplished in Christ Jesus our Lord* (Eph. 3:7-11, NIV).

These "rulers and authorities in the heavenly realms" are not the wicked host we see in Ephesians chapter six. These principalities are the heavenly hosts—all the saints who have gone on. Paul said that through the Church the manifold wisdom of God was going to be made known to them. Throughout his epistles Paul writes about this mystery of the Church that is going to be triumphant and take back what belongs to her. Jesus came to heal the brokenhearted, to set the captives free and to open the eyes of the blind. We have seen glimpses of that reality, but not as we will see it. The Church is going to have a revival that will not have men's names tagged on it, for Jesus Himself is going to be revealed in the Church.

At present, the Church is in a transitional period. The Charismatic era is coming to a close, not to be destroyed, but to be built upon. We are on the threshold of stepping into the last great era when we are going to have a mighty visitation of God and the Church will receive its inheritance. We will see the Church "grow up into him in all things, which is the head, even Christ: from whom the whole body fitly joined together and compacted by that which every joint supplieth, according to the effectual working in the measure of every part, maketh increase of the body unto the edifying of itself in love" (Eph. 4:15-16).

This move of God will include those of today's Joshua generation who are walking where He is walking, hearing what He is hearing, and moving where He is moving—not those who are merely attending church. Men and women of God all over the world are aware that the Church is in transition between the old move of God and the new move that is coming, when the Church will come into its inheritance and the Father will have a family that is conformed to the image of His Son.

Scripture is very clear regarding our responsibility as part of the Joshua generation who want to enter into our inheritance.

> *Every place that the sole of your foot shall tread upon, that have I given unto you . . . There shall not any man be able to stand before thee all the days of thy life: as I was with Moses, so I will be with thee: I will not fail thee, nor forsake thee. . . . This book of the law shall not depart out of thy mouth; but thou shalt meditate therein day and night, that thou mayest observe to do according to all that is written therein: for then thou shalt make thy way prosperous, and then thou shalt have good success* (Josh. 1:3,5,8).

Before the people of the new generation were ready to receive their inheritance, they had to be tested by life in the wilderness. God is training the Church through testings today. Some have taught that the saints aren't supposed to have trials and testings, but testings are necessary to reveal our lack of character and bring us to the place where we can receive His character. God doesn't test us to find out who we are, for He already knows that. We don't know who we are until God takes us through the testings and we see our response. The wilderness we are in is God's classroom. When it looks black and hopeless we may be tempted to think that God doesn't love us. To the contrary, He loves us so much He is training us to bring us to spiritual maturity so that we can receive our inheritance.

The first step to spiritual maturity is *crisis*. Crisis creates in us a *hunger*, which is the second step to maturity. Then follows a *searching* during which we receive *revelation*. Revelation brings us to *realization*, and we are able to enter into *service* and *obedience* in a mature walk in Christ. We will never find out how big our God is until we have to prove Him in crisis. He is not going to ask us to possess the land and war against the giants without first training us in the wilderness. He gives us grace every step of the way, carrying us as lambs in His bosom. Only those who have been fully sustained in their hearts through testings and trials can submit to Joshua's leadership. We must qualify, or be proven, to receive the inheritance.

As we have seen, "Canaan" does not refer to heaven, for there are no giants or "enemies" in heaven. The enemies inside us are the "ites" that hinder us from being changed into the image of God and thereby receiving our inheritance as a part of His family. We must conquer them in order to experience the love of God in the family of God. Contention, jealousy, outbursts of wrath, selfishness, ambitions, desires to rule, dissensions, heresies, envy, murder, drunkenness, and the like are all "ites" that keep us from our inheritance (Gal. 5:19-21). To run out the "ites" means to run out all forms of adultery as well, which is carrying on an affair with your own flesh, as well as with someone who does not belong to you. All fornication, uncleanness, hatred and unforgiveness must be purged from these temples of the Holy Ghost that Christ may receive glory in the Church, His body.

The Spirit of God is speaking regarding unforgiveness as I have never heard Him speak in my forty-one years of ministry. We must be forgiven of God and we must forgive everyone who has offended us. Recently my Father asked me to write to a certain minister to ask for his forgiveness. I can truthfully say I never did anything that I know of to hurt that minister. I esteemed him, even though through "prophecy" he had led a large number of my parishioners to leave the church I was pastoring. I felt that he was the one who had offended through that situation, and all I did in response was to stand aloof from him. But God dealt with that attitude in me and told me to ask the man's forgiveness for demanding innocence of him instead of being willing to accept his need to receive forgiveness.

I did what my Father asked, and through that obedience my temple was cleansed of one more "ite." A few weeks later, I was in awe at the new revelation that was flooding my own soul. As I was thanking God for it, He showed me that because of my obedience in writing that letter of forgiveness, a flow of power and truth had been released from the heavenlies to my own heart. God promises to equip us, and one by one we are going to overcome these enemies of our souls.

God's Church will march triumphantly into her inheritance. Do you think Jesus is not going to have what the Father planned? The Church is going to follow the example of Joshua and destroy the Hititomes, Girgashites, Canaanites, Hivites, Amalekites, "backbites," and all the other "ites" which are enemies that keep us from possessing our inheritance. My Father told me to go as a mother in Israel to help leaders to sharpen their swords and to prepare to take His people into the land of promise where God's dream will be fulfilled.

I thought that was the end of the message, but it wasn't. Some time later, my Teacher whispered to me that He wanted me to go back and read that passage in Joshua again because I had not seen everything He wanted me to see. He told me to look in the Book to see *when* Joshua was going into the land. I read, "Pass through the host, and command the people, saying, Prepare you victuals; for within three days ye shall pass over this Jordan, to go in to possess the land, which the Lord your God giveth you to possess it" (Josh. 1:11). God commanded Joshua to prepare the people, for in *three days* they were going to enter the land.

In Scripture, the word "day" can refer to twenty-four hours or to an era of time. Peter wrote, "But, beloved, be not ignorant of this one thing, that one day is with the Lord as a thousand years, and a thousand years as one day" (II Pet. 3:8). If we apply that principle to our calendar, we would say that in the year two thousand our second "day" is coming to a close, and we are about to enter the "third day" of our age. Our calendar is based on the history of the Church, the year one A.D. beginning after Christ's resurrection.

It is quite exciting to follow the mention of the "third day" throughout the Bible. For example, Esther went before the king on the third day of prayer and fasting to plead with him to save her and her people. Mordecai was able to pronounce the hanging of Haman on the third day. Jesus turned the water into wine on the third day at the wedding of Cana. And before He died, He said, "Destroy this temple and I will build it again in three days" (John 2:19). The Jews thought He meant Solomon's Temple, and we have thought He meant His own body. But He didn't build His own body—He is building the Church. He is the Head of the Church, which is His body. The prophet spoke in the Book of Hosea regarding the third day:

Come, and let us return unto the Lord: for he hath torn, and he will heal us; he hath smitten,

*and he will bind us up. After two days will he
revive us: in the third day he will raise us up,
and we shall live in his sight. Then shall we
know, if we follow on to know the Lord: his going
forth is prepared as the morning; and he shall
come unto us as the rain, as the latter and former
rain unto the earth* (Hos. 6:1-3).

People who are hearing the voice of God know
that He is going to do something soon. I said, "Now,
Lord, don't let me go out into left field by projecting
a time-table for Your moving." I don't know how long
the third day is going to last, but the Church is getting ready to enter the third day. Every time we
write the date we are saying the second day is coming to a close on our calendar. And we know the
Church is going into her inheritance, for Scripture
teaches that Jesus is coming for a glorious Church
without spot or wrinkle.

I was speaking at a convention in South Carolina
when the Holy Spirit told me He wanted me to see
something about the *first* day of the Church. So I went
back to the second chapter of Acts, where we see the
Church being baptized in the Holy Ghost. (The Church
was birthed on Resurrection day when Jesus breathed
upon His disciples.)

*And when the day of Pentecost was fully
come, they were all with one accord in one place.
And suddenly there came a sound from heaven*

*as of a rushing mighty wind, and it filled all the
house where they were sitting. And there ap-
peared unto them cloven tongues like as of fire,
and it sat upon each of them. And they were all
filled with the Holy Ghost, and began to speak
with other tongues, as the Spirit gave them ut-
terance* (Acts 2:1-4).

My attention was drawn to the phrase, "when the
day of Pentecost was fully come." The way it reads in
the original language is: "As the day dawned." Early in
the morning the Holy Ghost came and filled the one
hundred twenty people who were there in the upper
room. As that day dawned they all spoke in a tongue of
ecstasy, that is, an overflowing tongue that magnifies
God.

Then the Bible says, "Now when this was noised
abroad" (v. 6) a multitude came together of all those
nations that were visiting Jerusalem to celebrate the
Feast of Pentecost. All the noise the one hundred and
twenty were making at daybreak, speaking in tongues
of ecstasy, brought the attention of the multitude.
After that, the scene changed from the upper room to
the courtyard where the thousands had gathered to
see what the commotion was all about. And they were
all amazed because they heard these Galileans speaking in every language that was represented there (v. 6-
12). Peter refuted the idea that the disciples were
drunk, declaring, "these are not drunken as ye sup-
pose, seeing it is but the third hour of the day." At the

time he made that declaration, it was nine o'clock in the morning. The Holy Spirit had first come at the dawning of the day, when the day of Pentecost was "fully come." So the first day began when God came at the very dawning of the day to pour out His Holy Spirit on the Church. Then Peter preached the gospel to the representatives of the seventeen nations who were present that day, and three thousand souls were saved. What will God do at the dawning of the "third" day of the Church? We do not know, but let us live lives that are filled with the Holy Spirit so we can be part of God's moving.

In the literal history of the Book of Joshua, the people didn't ever receive all of their inheritance. They went into the promised land, but they married the "ites" instead of conquering them, and they never possessed the mountainous areas. "This time," God said to me, "the Church is not going to marry the 'ites.' She is going to possess the land." This is the greatest hour the Church has ever known. Our command now is to get our "vittles" ready, get our swords sharpened, come to maturity in Christ and let the Church be the Church.

The Father is going to bring the Church into that which the triune Godhead ordained before the foundation of the world. That intertheistic covenant that the Godhead swore together will not be broken, and no demon, devil, man or denomination will be able to keep the Son from receiving His inheritance. We must become that Church without spot or blemish, one mature man, growing up into our Head, which is Christ. Relating to the typology of Joshua, we must possess the land, conquering all the enemies of our souls, following our heavenly Joshua's battle plans, until we enter into all of our inheritance.

God had given me a life-changing message. It birthed a cry in the hearts of that graduating class to become a part of the new generation, and many of them are serving on foreign mission fields today. This message is consuming me as I travel across the nation to fulfill the mandate of God to help prepare His leaders and His people to come into their inheritance. It is a message that can be life-changing for everyone who believes the eternal plan of God. All who dare to respond to the working of the Holy Spirit will find themselves becoming a wonderful part of fulfilling God's dream.